The Ultimate Italian Cookbook

Diana Vowles

CHARTWELL
BOOKS, INC.

D1300417

A QUANTUM BOOK

This edition published in 2011 by

CHARTWELL BOOKS, INC.

A division of BOOK SALES, INC.

276 Fifth Avenue, Suite 206

New York, New York 10001

USA

ISBN-13: 978-0-7858-2849-5

QUMTUIC

This book is produced by

Quantum Publishing

6 Blundell Street

London N7 9BH

Digitized by Quadrum Solutions, Mumbai, Indian

www.quadrumltd.com

Cover design by Dave Jones, www.euro-designs.info

Consultant Editors: Diana Vowles and Caroline Smith

Managing Editor: Julie Brooke

Project Editor: Samantha Warrington

Assistant Editor: Jo Morley

Production Manager: Rohana Yusof

Publisher: Sarah Bloxham

Printed in Singapore by

Star Standard Industries Pte Ltd

The material in this publication previously appeared in *Complete Italian Cookbook*,

Italian Regional Cooking, Italian Trattoria, Cooking with Pasta and *The Pasta and Pizza Cookbook*

Contents

The Origins of Italian Cooking

Italian food is the mother of all European cuisine, a fact acknowledged by even the *Larousse Gastronomique*. Its origins are well recorded by the writers of ancient Rome, who left very vivid impressions of the orgies indulged in by the ruling classes – but this is only half of the picture.

For while the aristocracy sat down, or rather reclined, to such dishes as peacock dressed in all its feathers or boar stuffed with live thrushes, the common soldier was roasting his ration of millet on a stone set in the campfire. When it was done, he crushed it, boiled it up with water and ate it as gruel. What was left over solidified into a cake and was consumed cold. This primitive meal was called *pulmentum,* and it has survived right up to the present day in the tastier form of polenta, whereas the more excessive dishes of the Empire, though more memorable, declined and fell with it.

Though what endured was, like polenta, deeply rooted in peasant life, the extravagance of Imperial tables is impossible to ignore. Flamingos and herons were also served up in their plumage; hedgehogs, puppies, wolves and donkeys enjoyed a great popularity; dormice were kept in a barrel to stop them losing weight by exercise and were fed until they were fat, then roasted in honey and herbs. A favorite banquet recipe was "Trojan pork". The title referred to the Horse of Troy, which had concealed the ambushing Greek soldiers. Trojan pork was stuffed with oysters and songbirds. One side of it was smeared with meal soaked in wine and oil and roasted, then the pig was turned over and the uncooked side was dipped into boiling water until it was done. Among the more exotic delicacies of the day were camel's foot and elephant's trunk.

All these things were consumed in stupendous quantities by the few who could afford them. The Emperor Maximinius is reputed to have eaten over 18 kg (40 lb) of meat a day, and to have drunk 20 liters (35 pt) of wine. The Emperor Aurelian commissioned an actor, Farone, to amuse him by eating in one session a whole sheep, a whole suckling pig and a whole boar, accompanied by 100 rolls and 100 bottles of wine.

The ancient Romans were fond of cooking with all the herbs and spices to which their vast empire gave them access. The original Roman seasoning was salt, evaporated from the water at the mouth of the River Tiber. It was used as a preservative for meat, and when more was made than could be used at home it became the basis for Rome's first important export trade, carried out of the city along the Via Salaria – the Salt Road – which remains to this day.

To make salted meat more palatable, the Romans later added honey, dried fruit and spices. The resulting taste was the ancestor of today's *agrodolce,* a bittersweet sauce enjoyed with many different foods, including game and cabbage. A less attractive flavoring that seems to have been used liberally to disguise the taste of salt meat was *garum,* which one writer described as a sauce made from the entrails of mackerel.

Poultry could be reared by every household and there was a plentiful supply of chickens from Roman markets. Guinea fowl, pigeon and duck were also popular, and when the Romans conquered Gaul they discovered a great liking for goose. Consequently the returning troops drove huge flocks of geese from Picardy to Rome, living off the fields and causing much devastation as they went.

During the 2nd century the Emperor Trajan built the Forum, and next to it on Quirinal Hill a supermarket, a semicircular structure with both open-air and closed booths (see opposite). Behind

Above: Trajan's Market in the present day, a complex of ruins in the city of Rome, Italy.

it rambled multistory buildings housing more shops and stalls. There the Romans bought and sold meat, poultry, fish and wine. Olive oil was imported from Spain, wheat from Egypt and spices from Asia.

Cabbage was grown by the better off, while the poor ate beans, mallow and a species of nettle. Spinach was not known until the 9th century, when it was introduced from Persia. Persia also provided Italy with melons, which farmers began to cultivate at Cantalupo, outside Rome. Figs and wild cherries were highly prized natives.

Honey was used as a sweetener – even on savory foods. The Roman dish of honeyed eggs, *ova mellita*, gave its name to today's omelet. Another food given the sweet treatment was cheese. Flour and crushed fresh cheese were mixed with honey and eggs and baked in an earthenware mold – the cheesecake was born. The crushed fresh cheese in question was the ancestor of ricotta, but the Romans had a dozen varieties of cheese, of which they were very fond.

In the 3rd century AD, Rome fell to the barbarians and the excesses of the degenerate empire were replaced by a more sober lifestyle. Recipes were preserved, as were other writings, in monasteries. In the 9th century came the Islamic invasion, which brought a new injection of life into Italian cooking. The Arabs brought with them the techniques of making ice cream and sorbet, and introduced desserts and sweet cakes made with marzipan. They were also responsible for planting the first sugar cane in Europe, but its cultivation did not really catch on until 200 years later, when cane and refined sugar were brought back by the Crusaders. Sugar went by the name of "Indian salt" and was used as salt was, to season fish and meat. The Crusaders also reintroduced the spices that had been known in the days of ancient Rome, and a new interest in cooking sprang up. Milk and egg pies, vegetable tarts and bread sweetened with dried fruit appeared in a recipe book around 1290, along with the first ever mention of pasta.

When Marco Polo opened up the spice trade between Venice and the Far East, Venetians grew fat on the profits and Venice became a center of gastronomy. It was there that the table fork became popular and that drinking vessels were first made of fine glass.

In 16th-century Florence the first modern cooking academy was set up. Called *Compagnia del Paiolo* (Company of the Cauldron), one of its members was the painter Andrea del Sarto, who presented his colleagues with an exhibition dish made of gelatin in the shape of a temple held up by pillars of sausages and Parmesan. Inside was a book with pages of pasta, and in front stood roasted thrushes, singing notes inscribed on the pasta in peppercorns.

In 1533 Catherine de Medici journeyed from Florence to France to marry the future King Henri II. France was still in the dark ages as far as the art of cooking was concerned, and Catherine took her own chefs and pastry cooks, who were adept at making ices, cakes and cream puffs. Marie de Medici followed in her footsteps in 1600 to become the bride of Henri IV. The Florentines were responsible for introducing navy beans, peas, broccoli, artichokes and savoy cabbage to the French, and they also educated them in the culinary skills that were soon to make their own cuisine great and renowned the world over.

From Italy too came the double boiler. The French adopted it as the *bain marie*, but the original Mary's bath or *bagno maria* was named after its inventor Maria de Cleofsa, an alchemist who devised it to help her with her arcane research into the relationship between magic, medicine and cooking.

The 16th century saw the arrival of the first tomato in Italy, brought back to Europe with the first red pepper from Mexico by the Spanish conquistadors. Called the *pomo d'oro* (golden apple), it was a cherry-sized yellow fruit used as a salad vegetable. It took 200 years for the large luscious red varieties to be developed for use in cooking.

Coffee was imported from the East. In 1585 Venice's ambassador to Turkey described to the Senate "the habit of the Turks of drinking a black water as hot as you can bear it, taken from seeds called cavee, and they say it has the power of keeping men awake". Its popularity was quickly established in Venice and soon spread all across Europe.

The arrival of the potato was greeted with less enthusiasm. Pope Clement VII's botanist classified the specimen presented to him as "a small truffle" and henceforward it was cultivated in Italian gardens – as a decorative plant. The Italians were not alone in their confusion as to what to do with the potato – Queen Elizabeth I's chef threw away the tubers and served up the leaves. Potatoes never became a staple in Italy, even when their true use was discovered. Corn, the last major import, which came from America, provided a more popular alternative form of starch.

By the 16th century, the French had become so advanced in the art of cooking that chefs from the French court were sent back to Venice to demonstrate their skills. The Venetians were not impressed. "French cooks have ruined the Venetian stomach," wrote Gerolamo Zanetti, "with so much *porchere* (filth) ... sauces, broths, essences ... garlic and onion in every dish ... meat and fish transformed to such a point that they are scarcely recognizable by the time they get to the table ... Everything mashed and mixed up with a hundred herbs, spices, sauces …"

Though the author was a biased (Venetian) observer writing some 400 years ago, his comment serves to underline the major difference between present-day Italian and French cooking. For while French cuisine tends to be elaborate and subtle, that of Italy is bold, simple and direct. Zanetti's

Above: The artist Longlin's depiction of a sumptuous 18th-century banquet, held in Venice in honor of the visiting Elector of Cologne.

mistrust of foreigners' meddling with good basic ingredients, transforming them into something "scarcely recognizable", also shows a fierce respect for local tradition that is very much a part of Italian cooking today. It is not just influence from abroad that is resisted, but influence from other regions of Italy, and it is this that makes Italian cooking so varied and unique.

The Flavors of Italy

Italian cooking is the cooking of its regions. Until 1861 the regions of Italy were separate and often hostile states. Geographically as well as politically isolated from each other, they developed their own distinctive culinary character and traditions – traditions that are fiercely and proudly preserved today.

In Italy what is local is best. An Emilian would regard a salami produced in neighboring Tuscany with skepticism; a Tuscan might smile ruefully at the Emilian's extravagant use of butter and cream. It follows that the traveler intent on enjoying Italian food should always order what the locals eat. It is no good asking for *osso buco* in Naples or *bistecca* in Genoa, as they will be but pale imitations of the genuine things to be had in Milan and Florence – and you will have missed the opportunity to sample the perfect *spaghetti alla marinara* and *torta pasqualina*.

Italian pride in local fare and disdain of "imports", be they from only a few miles away, is soundly rooted in a love of fresh food. If there is one aspect of cooking shared by all the regions of Italy, it is the importance placed on the quality of the ingredients. Fruit and vegetables must be homegrown, preferably without chemical fertilizers, and picked at the peak of ripeness and glossy perfection. A squeeze of lemon juice is known to have more zest when the lemon is freshly picked from the tree and still warm from the sun, than when it has traveled long distances, ripening slowly in a crate. Meat should be home reared and home killed, and fish straight from the catch – seafood is rarely served at any distance from the coast.

All over Italy, Italians treat their food with respect. Their cooking is designed to emphasize the natural flavors of the ingredients. In this it is very different from French cooking, with its subtle harmonies and sophisticated sauces. Italian food is brightly colored when it reappears on the plate. It is good, wholesome, hearty and endlessly varied – essentially home cooking that requires very few skills to master.

The main meal in Italy is eaten in the middle of the day and can consist of several courses. First there may be a soup. This is usually a clear broth made substantial with rice or pasta, grated vegetables or the dumplings made of potato or semolina called gnocchi. An alternative to soup would be a risotto or a dish of baked or boiled pasta with a piquant or creamy sauce. Generous helpings of freshly grated Parmesan cheese top this first course. Next comes a dish of fish or meat. In some areas the meat would be quite plainly cooked, perhaps grilled with aromatic olive oil and herbs as its only added flavoring; in others it might be a more complicated dish layered with melting cheese and tender ham coated in breadcrumbs and fried in pork fat until succulent and golden.

A *contorno* – literally a contour – of seasonal vegetables or salad can be served with or after this course. To finish with, there will be fruit and local cheese, and the meal is of course accompanied by the wine of the region.

On Sundays or special occasions lunch may begin with *antipasti* – a selection of salami, fish, olives, artichokes and other savory appetizers both hot and cold – and end with one of Italy's famous desserts, ices, cakes or pastries and black espresso coffee and liqueurs.

The Regions of Italy

The regions listed below represent the main geographical divisions of Italy. The shields shown are those of the main town or city in each region.

Key to regions

Piedmont
(see p.14)

Veneto
(see p.16)

Lombardy
(see p.18)

Liguria
(see p.19)

Emilia-Romagna
(see p.20)

Tuscany
(see p.22)

Lazio, Umbria and
The Marches
(see p.24)

Naples and the South
(see p.26)

Sicily
(see p.27)

Sardinia
(see p.27)

Key to wine areas

1. Piedmont, see p.14.
2. Veneto, see p.16.
3. Friuli–Venezia Giulia, see p.17.
4. Trentino-Alto Adige, see p.17.
5. Lombardy, see p.18.
6. Liguria, see p.19.
7. Emilia-Romagna, see p.20.
8. Tuscany, see p.22.
9. Lazio, see p.24.
10. Umbria and The Marches, see p.24.
11. Abruzzi-Molise, see p.26.
12. Campania, see p.26.
13. Basilicata, see p.26.
14. Apulia, see p.26.
15. Calabria, see p.26.
16. Sicily, see p.27.
17. Sardinia, see p.27.

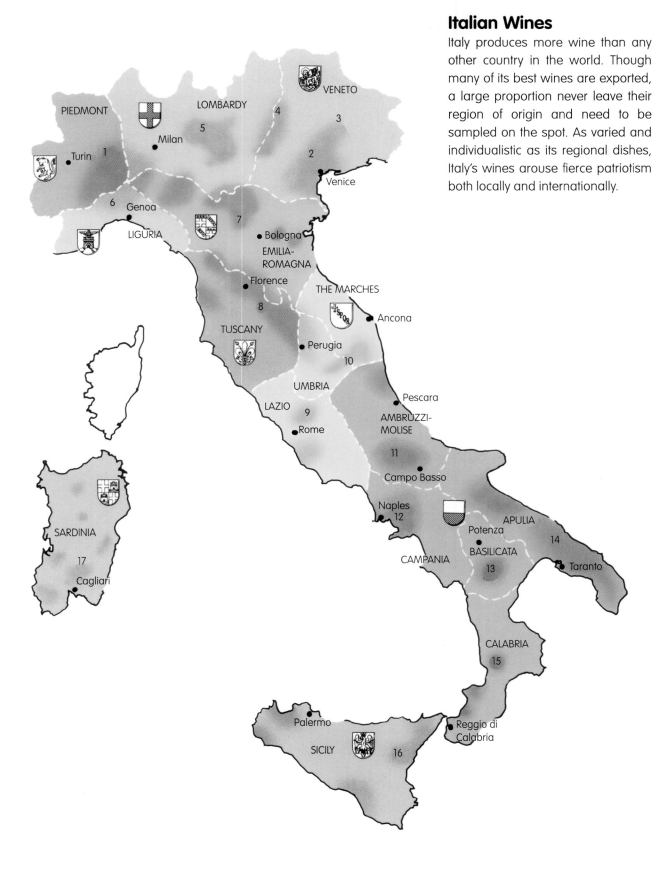

PIEDMONT

LOMBARDY

VENETO

4

5

3

Milan

2

Turin

1

Venice

6 Genoa

7

LIGURIA

Bologna

EMILIA-
ROMAGNA

Florence

THE MARCHES

8

Ancona

TUSCANY

Perugia

10

UMBRIA

LAZIO

Pescara

9

AMBRUZZI-
MOLISE

Rome

11

Campo Basso

Naples

12

APULIA

Potenza

14

SARDINIA

BASILICATA

17

CAMPANIA

13

Taranto

Cagliari

CALABRIA

15

Palermo

Reggio di
Calabria

SICILY

16

Italian Wines

Italy produces more wine than any other country in the world. Though many of its best wines are exported, a large proportion never leave their region of origin and need to be sampled on the spot. As varied and individualistic as its regional dishes, Italy's wines arouse fierce patriotism both locally and internationally.

Piedmont

Piedmont is a mainly mountainous region and, as in other places with similar upland terrains, its diet is hearty, substantial and sustaining. However, its capital, Turin, also has a long tradition of culinary sophistication inherited from its great ruling House of Savoy, and this gives Piedmontese cooking a special edge of distinction that is lacking in other mountain areas. Robust peasant dishes of lasagne, polenta, gnocchi and boiled mixed meats are to be found side by side delicacies such as trout baked on a bed of mushrooms, and the famous *bagna cauda*, which is a hot sauce of olive oil, butter, garlic and pounded anchovies. The latter is eaten as a dip for a variety of cold vegetables, among which is often the cardoon, or edible thistle.

Another delicious Piedmontese speciality is *fonduta*. This is a kind of fondue made with fat fontina cheese, cornstarch, milk and egg yolks, which is sometimes served poured over a slab of polenta and decorated with finely sliced truffles.

The frogs that breed prolifically in the Piedmontese rice fields are served up, appropriately enough, in risotto. Indeed, as Piedmont is the main rice growing region of Italy, it would be suprising if rice did not feature heavily in Piedmontese cuisine. Another notable culinary feature of the area is that every meal is accompanied by *grissini*, the long crisp breadsticks that have become synonymous with Italian eating throughout the world. For desserts you might be offered a rich confection of chestnuts and cream called *monte bianco*, and after the meal a glass of grappa.

The Wines of Piedmont

Fine wines have been grown in Piedmont since Roman times. This is possible as the vineyards are gently sloping, the sun is not too fierce, and the vines are protected from the wind by the Alps. Most of the region's wine is full-bodied red, but it also produces the sparkling white Asti Spumante, the favorite of many. Turin is the center of vermouth production, which mostly uses the cheaper wine of Aplilia. The vermouth's aroma comes from the herbs that grow in the nearby mountains.

ASTI SPUMANTE

A sparkling, sweet white wine made from the Moscato grape, which is widely grown in Piedmont, Asti is made by the *cuvé close* method - fermented in closed vats and bottled under pressure. This is quicker and cheaper than the *méthode champagnoise*, which involves secondary fermentation in the bottle, and which is also used in this region to produce some sparkling dry whites, for example Gancia Royal Cuvée. Asti is a classic dessert wine that can also be enjoyed mid-morning or at parties.

BARBARESCO

A full-bodied, deep red wine made from the Nebbiolo grape, it matures early, taking on a slight amber tint. It comes from the hilly country near Alba.

BARBERA

Piedmont's commonest wine, this is a red that can vary greatly in quality. It can be slightly sparkling and sweet; it can be rather coarse when young but will acquire a mellow flavor with age. The best Barbera, which comes from around Asti, is granted a growers' association label of blue grapes on the city's red tower.

BAROLO

One of Italy's great wines, Barolo is deep red when young and takes on an amber tinge with age. It is made from the Nebbiolo grape grown in the hills around Alba and is full and fragrant with a hint of violets. Barolo is particularly enjoyable with snails, game and mature cheese.

CORTESE DELL'ALTO MONFERRATO

A light, dry white to be drunk young with fish.
A semi-sweet sparkling version is called Cortese
di Gavi.

FREISA

A smooth, dry, garnet-red wine from near Turin. It has
a hint of raspberries and violets.

GATTINARA

A highly prized garnet-red wine with a hint of
raspberries, Gattinara is preferred to Barolo by some
connoisseurs. Made from the aristocratic Nebbiolo
grape, it is best after three years in the bottle.

GRIGNOLINO D'ASTI

Rose-colored and perfumed, from the Grignolino
grape, this is a wine to be drunk young and cool with
pasta or poultry.

MOSCATO D'ASTI

A cheaper, commoner version of Asti Spumante.

PASSITO DI CALUSO

A golden-yellow dessert wine, full, round and fruity,
made from Erbulace grapes that have been partly dried
in the sun after picking to concentrate their sweetness.
Excellent with fresh white cheese.

Veneto

Veneto, with Trentio to the west and Friuli-Venezia Giulia to the east, is one of Italy's major wine-producing areas and its famous exports include Soave, Valpolicella and Bardolino. Its gastronomic center is its capital, Venice, whose cuisine still reflects the legacy of the medieval spice trade. Here you can enjoy lightly curried fish and a delicate dish of peppered calf's liver and onions. The Venetians' taste is, on the whole, exotic. They like rice with *scampi* (jumbo shrimp), squid or shrimp in a garlic and tomato sauce, and even rice with grapes, cheese and garlic. Salt cod is cooked with cinnamon, turkey with pomegranate sauce and zucchini flowers are fried in butter.

Pasta is not often eaten in Veneto. Instead the locals favor polenta, which is not yellow as in most other parts of Italy, but white, made from the fine white corn grown in Friuli-Venezia Giulia. Another simple dish prized by the Venetians is *risi e bisi*, rice and peas. This falls somewhere between a soup and a risotto and is at its best with the tender young peas available only in spring.

The merchants of Venice first introduced sugar into Europe and Venetians today still have a sweet tooth. In the middle of the morning the city is full of people sitting under awnings enjoying their *ombrina* – "little shade" – a glass of wine or a cup of coffee and sweet cornmeal biscuits or the vanilla cake called *pandoro*.

The Wines of Veneto

One of the major wine growing regions, Veneto produces Valpolicella, Bardolino and Soave, three of Italy's best-known exports.

BARDOLINO
A bright, ruby-red wine with a fresh taste, made from a variety of grapes grown on the eastern shores of Lake Garda. Best drunk young and cool.

CABERNET
A full-bodied, vigorous red with a slight amber tint, best after it has spent at least three years in the bottle.

COLLI DI VALDOBBIADENE
A dry white with a hint of bitterness, and a sweet, slightly sparkling dessert wine, both bear this name.

MERLOT
A ruby-red wine with a fresh taste and a hint of almond. The Merlot grape is grown all over Italy; the Veneto Merlot is lighter than that from Trentino.

PROSECCO
A straw-yellow wine, aromatic and fresh. There is also a sparkling variety – Prosecco Spumante. Prosecco is grown all over the north of Italy.

RABOSO
A rather rough red wine common across the region, and best drunk young.

RECIOTO
A red wine, so called as it is made only from the "ears" (orecchie) of the bunches of grapes, which are riper than the rest. It is full and heavy and makes a good accompaniment to roasted meat and mature cheese.

SOAVE
Smooth, dry and straw-yellow, this is one of the finest Italian whites. It is made mainly from Garganega grapes and is best drunk young and chilled as an accompaniment to the fish dishes of Venice.

VALPOLICELLA
Slightly fuller than Bardolino, this is the most popular red of the region. It can be aged in the bottle, but is perhaps best drunk cool and young.

The Wines of Friuli-Venezia Giulia

The character of this region is more Slavic than Italian and the inhabitants are less patriotic than anywhere else in Italy. You are as likely to be served a Yugoslavian wine in Veneto as one grown locally.

GAMAY

A brilliant ruby-red wine from vines imported from France. Gamay grows well on the hills of the region and has a faint strawberry taste when young.

PICCOLIT

A golden-yellow dessert wine drunk chilled. It was much admired in European courts at the turn of the century and is best when it has aged a few years in the bottle. Piccolit grapes are part dried in the sun after being picked to give the wine a more concentrated sweetness.

PINOT GRIGIO

Arguably the best white wine of the region, it has a slightly pink tinge and a faint tang of nutmeg. There are also smooth red and spumante versions.

SAUVIGNON

Another grape imported from France and grown widely throughout the region. An elegant, straw-yellow wine with a slightly bitter aftertaste.

TOCAI

A dry yellow-white wine quite unlike the Hungarian Tokay, which is a great dessert wine. Makes a very good accompaniment to fish dishes.

The Wines of Trentino-Alto Adige

Alto Adige, which its inhabitants call the South Tyrol, is German speaking, and the wines have German names and are exported to Germany, Switzerland and Austria. The wines are finer and quite distinct from those produced in Trentino, which are less numerous.

BLAUBURGUNDER

A reliable, full red wine from the Pinot Noir grape grown around Bolzano, Caldaro and Terlano.

CALDARO

Lugadi Caldaro is a full red wine with a slight almond flavor. Often called Kalterersee, the German name for the lake.

COLLINE BOLZANO

Red wines from the Schiavone grapes grown on the hills around Bolzano. Variable in quality.

GEWÜRZTRAMINER

In the South Tyrol is the village of Tramin, or Termeno, which the locals claim gave Gewürztraminer its name. But the white wine from this region is not as full or fragrant as its more famous namesake from Alsace.

RIESLING

A well balanced wine, the Terlaner Riesling is one of the few whites of the area that are exported.

SANTA MAGDALENA

The finest red wine of this region – a brilliant ruby with a hint of orange, it is smooth with a slightly bitter aftertaste. Made from Schiava and Schiavone grapes, and grown in the hills east of Bolzano.

Lombardy

Lombardy's national dish is *risotto alla milanese*, rice delicately flavored and colored with saffron. Another speciality is *osso buco*, braised veal shank on the bone, of which the marrow is considered to be the tastiest part. To the Milanese goes the credit of inventing another famous meat dish, the *wiener schnitzel*. The original *costoletta alla milanese*, the breaded veal chop, was taken back to Vienna in the 19th century by General Radetzky, and the Viennese promptly adopted them as their own.

Milan is Italy's financial capital and though the pace of life there is fast, cooking methods are traditionally slow and housewives spend long hours at the stove, braising, stewing, spit roasting and gently simmering meat to succulent perfection. It is generally held in France that the Italians overcook their meat, and they certainly like it well done.

Though Lombardy is famous for its rice, it does not grow quite as much of it as Piedmont. It is primarily an area of wheat and dairy farming. Butter is the cooking medium and there are some excellent cheeses, among them Gorgonzola. In Milan is the Via dei Ghiottoni, the street of gourmets (or gluttons), which is lined with food shops of every possible type. One in particular, called Peck, is internationally renowned for its enormous selection of cheeses and its top quality veal and cured meats. One of the more unusual of these is *bresaola*, beef salted and dried and sliced paper thin to be eaten with olive oil, lemon juice and pepper.

Every visitor to Milan is sure to be offered a slice of panettone, a leavened cake made with eggs, raisins and candied peel that is the ideal breakfast accompaniment to a cup of coffee. Torrone is an almond-flavored dessert that has been a popular treat since the 13th century, and another favorite dessert is pears stuffed with Gorgonzola cheese.

The Wines of Lombardy

In the Valtelline, with the Alps to the north and the mountains of Bergamo to the south, the aristocratic Nebbiolo produces fine red wines as in Piedmont – Sassella, Grumello and Inferno. But they are quite elusive and inconsistent in quality and are often exported to Switzerland or appear under a brand name. The other main wine producing areas are around Lake Garda and to the south of the river Po in the Oltrepo Pavese.

CHIARETTO DEL GARDA

The red wines around Lake Garda are very light, and the rosés darker than the French ones. This is an intense pink wine made from a mixture of four types of grape. It has a sharp fresh taste and should be drunk young and cool. It is a good wine to choose for an outdoor lunch.

Liguria

This is the narrow strip of coast that stretches from San Remo to La Spezia and is bordered to the north by the Alps and Apennines. Its capital is the great port of Genoa and its culinary traditions, not surprisingly, reflect the seafaring nature of its inhabitants. For the fishermen who spent weeks at sea, food had to be prepared to keep. Pulses, chickpeas and dried beans, pies and cookies were eaten at sea and when they returned home, the sailors satisfied their cravings for fresh green vegetables with tarts filled with artichokes, spinach, zucchini, Swiss chard and wild herbs – *torta pasqualina*. Genoa's favorite herb is basil, the main ingredient for pesto sauce. The word comes from "pestle." Basil, garlic, Parmesan, olive oil and pine nuts – and sometimes lemon peel, beans and potatoes – are pounded together with a pestle in a mortar and served with gnocchi or pasta.

The land of Liguria is not good farming land, so every little bit of vegetation must be put to good use. One recipe calls for wild herbs, "the kind you find growing on the garden wall." Ligurian frugality was responsible for the invention of ravioli – the word comes from *robiole*, or leftovers – little offcuts stuffed into envelopes of pasta. *Cappon magro* is a true Genoese joke. Literally "thin capon," it is a dish that contains no meat at all. It is, for all that, a very majestic concoction and has been pronounced worthy of Homeric heroes. Layered boiled vegetables and pickled fish are built up to form a huge colorful dome which is then draped in a green sauce flavored with herbs.

The Wines of Liguria

Liguria is a small region and an even smaller wine producer, with most of the vineyards growing enough to supply only their owners' tables. Genoa is the center of the Italian wine trade, but it deals in the wines of the rest of Italy and drinks its own at home.

BARBAROSSA

So called because of the way the grape grows in "red beards." A festive pink wine, there is also a sweet variety.

CAMPOCHIESA BIANCO

A full-flavored dry white wine from the Pigato grape, Campochiesa improves with age. Traditionally it is laid down at the birth of a son to be drunk at his wedding.

CINQUETERRE

Drunk young, this is a delicate, clear, yellow-gold wine with a slightly bitter taste, made from the Vernaccia grape. It comes from five villages – hence its name – high up in rocky terrain. There is a sweet variety made from grapes part dried in the sun. It has a high alcohol content (16 percent) and is much enjoyed with ice cream.

CORONATA

A dry white wine with a sharp, fresh taste that goes very well with fish.

DOLCEACQUA

Made mainly from Rosesse grapes, this is a full, heavy aromatic wine that goes well with stronger-flavored local dishes, such as pesto.

Emilia-Romagna

This rich and fertile region lying to the north of Tuscany is Italy's land of plenty, and its capital, Bologna, is known as *Bologna la grassa* – "the fat." Bologna is the home of *mortadella*, perhaps Italy's finest sausage, and, above all, fresh pasta. Made from local wheat milled very finely, bolognese pasta is rolled out so thinly you can almost see through it, cut into long narrow strips to make tagliatelle and served with a tasty ragu, which comes from the French word *ragoût*, or stew. It is said that the inventor of tagliatelle was inspired by the fine flaxen hair of Lucretia Borgia and that the inventor of tortellini, little stuffed rings of pasta, fell in love with his employer's wife when he saw her sleeping in the nude and promptly produced a new pasta in the shape of her navel.

Tortellini stuffed with turkey, sausage, ham, pork, egg and cheese are traditionally served on Christmas Day as a first course with a rich sauce of butter and cream and topped with grated cheese. Lasagne, baked in the oven with layers of meat and cream sauces, and cappelletti, "little hats," stuffed with ricotta, chicken, egg and spices, are other popular forms of pasta in Bologna.

Emilians are very fond of veal and serve it in their typically extravagant way, stuffed with cheese and ham and braised in wine, a habit that would horrify their plainer-living Tuscan neighbors.

In Emilia is the city of Parma, renowned throughout the world for its prosciutto or Parma ham, and for having given its name to Parmesan cheese. The original Parmesan is made in Reggio nell'Emilia and is known variously as parmigiano reggiano or formaggio di grana, "grained cheese," because of its finely grained texture. It is probably the cheese most closely identified with Italian cuisine.

From Modena comes *zampone*, stuffed foreleg of pork, and from Piacenza *bomba di riso*, a dessert-shaped mold of rice cooked in white wine that contains vegetables and pigeons cooked in red wine. In Ferrara the local delicacy is grilled eel and at Ravenna you can sample another Italian fish soup, *brodetto*.

The Wines of Emilia-Romagna

The wines of this region are not as full and flavorsome as its cooking. Its most famous wine is Lambrusco, a dry sparkling red, beloved by the Bolognese and arousing strong reactions in visitors from outside the region, who are either captivated or repelled.

ALBANA

A well balanced, yellow-gold wine grown around the town of Bertinoro. Light and fresh with a slight sweetness, but nevertheless delicious with fish.

CASTELFRANCO

A fragrant dry white wine from near Modena, made from a mixture of grapes grown in the same vineyard.

GUTTURNIO

A dryish, ruby-red wine, best drunk very young and served cool, made mainly from Barbera grapes.

LAMBRUSCO

Dry, red and sparkling, very pink and frothy when poured, but the bubbles subside to a tingle. The Bolognese say that its fresh, clean taste complements their rich cooking and that it aids digestion.

SANGIOVESE

A fresh, ruby-red wine with a hint of garnet, widely grown throughout the region. Fruity when young, it mellows with age and is prized by the locals.

SCANDIANO BIANCO

A popular, straw-yellow wine, this is not renowned for its quality outside the region. There are dry and sparkling sweet varieties.

TREBBIANO

This grape is widely grown in the region, producing wines of different style and quality. The more common variety is drunk young, but there is also a sharp elegant wine that goes well with fish and a sweeter sparkling Trebbiano for dessert.

Tuscany

Tuscany is the heart of Italy. Its food is simply prepared with the best ingredients. Elaborate dishes have no place on the menu here; indeed the Tuscan way of cooking is sometimes looked upon by outsiders as austere because of its conspicuous lack of complicated sauces and seasonings.

Florence is the capital and, in culinary terms, Florentine (*alla fiorentina*) is synonymous with spinach. But this is only outside Italy – to an Italian *alla fiorentina* simply means "in the Florentine style." *Bistecca alla fiorentina* is a typical Tuscan dish well worth travelling miles to sample in its native city – it is simply prepared with ingredients of the highest quality, and it does not contain spinach. It is steak from a choice two-year-old Chana Valley bull, that is grilled briefly above chestnut wood. It is salted and rubbed with a little olive oil just before it is removed from the fire and served perhaps with fresh beans.

Tuscans are known throughout Italy as *mangiafagioli* (bean eaters). They eat beans in soup, beans in risotto and beans with pasta. Beans and tuna fish is a favorite appetizer. *Fagioli nel fiasco* is beans cooked slowly in a closed flask to prevent the flavor from escaping. They are then eaten simply with olive oil, salt, pepper and lemon juice and Tuscan bread.

The bread in Tuscany is unsalted, as it forms a part of so many dishes that a too-salty flavor would ruin. There is, for example, a bread salad, tossed with tomatoes, cucumber and red onions, and a bread and tomato soup, especially beloved by children. The other reason that bread is not salted is that salt absorbs moisture, and bread is bought in big enough quantities to last a week. Salted bread would go moldy before the week was out. The Tuscans are a practical and economy-conscious people.

They are very fond of game, particularly pheasant and hare, which is plentiful in the hillsides, and which they serve simply roasted and flavored with wild rosemary. Their pecorino cheese with its sharp flavor and black crust is one of the best in Italy and is an excellent accompaniment to Chianti, Tuscany's famous wine.

There are two more specialities of the region that deserve a mention – Livorno's splendid fish soup, *cacciucco alla livornese*, and Siena's flat dessert, *panforte*, full of dried fruit, almonds and spices, often taken home by tourists as a souvenir of the lovely medieval city that makes it.

The Wines of Tuscany

The landscape of Tuscany used to reflect the diet of its inhabitants: bread, olive oil and wine. Corn, olive trees and vines would be grown in the same field, with perhaps a cow or two wandering among them. The peasants had to give half of their produce to the landowners and could not risk a single crop. Now the wines have taken over in rows well spaced enough to allow the passage of a tractor. Still, a few farmers have kept their olive trees, as much because the grey-green color is a vital part of landscape as for their oil.

ARBIA

A dry white wine that goes well with the pecorino – sheep's cheese – of the region. A "virgin" wine, as the must is fermented without stalks or skin.

BRUNELLO DI MONTALCINO

One of the great Italian reds – full and fragrant, smooth and well balanced, it is aged in the cask for five or six years and enthusiasts recommend keeping it in the bottle for up to 50 years.

CANDIA

Sweet red and white wines from the northwest of the region.

CHIANTI

Baron Bertino Ricasoli "invented" Chianti in the 1860s. When his young wife danced at a ball with a man who seemed to be paying her too much attention, he called her away and they drove all night to Brolio, where there was a gloomy castle the baron's family had not lived in for years. Here they set up a permanent home well away from the temptations of society. The baron diverted himself by developing a new wine – a mixture of black Sangiovese and white Malvasia grapes, and a method of making them ferment twice, giving the wine a novel taste and a slight tingle. When the first fermentation is over, a rich must from dried grapes is added to the wine, inducing a second fermentation that lasts from two to three weeks. Wines made by this method are drunk young and sold in typical Chianti flasks covered in wicker (or plastic). Finer Chiantis meant to be aged are only fermented once and sold in ordinary bottles. Chianti is produced and exported on a very large scale, but Chianti classico comes only from the area between Florence and Siena and bears the growers' label of a black rooster against a gold background.

MOSCADELLO DI MONTALCINO

A light, golden fragrant wine with a slight tingle, drunk young and chilled.

UGOLINO BIANCO

A clear straw-colored white from near Livorno. To be drunk young and chilled with fish.

VAL DI CHIANA

A clear, golden-yellow wine; a "virgin" like Arbia, see left.

VERNACCIA DI SAN GIMIGNANO

A fresh, straw-colored wine with a hint of bitterness comes from around this picturesque town, which has been completely overtaken by tourism. It is a fine, dry white that improves with age.

VIN NOBILE DI MONTEPULCIANO

A smooth, well balanced ruby-red wine with a hint of violets, best after at least five years in the bottle.

VIN SANTO

A rich, sweet dessert wine, very popular in Tuscany.

Lazio, Umbria and The Marches

This central band across the knee of Italy is dominated by the capital, Rome. The Roman appetite is robust and hearty, and the food that satisfies it is both good and simple. Suckling pig stuffed with herbs and roasted on a spit is a typical favorite dish. The Roman gastronomical calendar moves from festival to festival, with roast capon at Christmas, stuffed with breadcrumbs, salami, giblets and cheese; suckling lamb at Easter; and on Midsummer Night, snails in a sauce of garlic, anchovy, tomato and mint.

In Rome you can eat both the fresh homemade pasta of the north, in a justly famous dish of cannelloni – flat pasta sheets rolled around a meat filling – and the dried tubular pasta of the south. Sauces include tuna and mushrooms (*alla carrettiera*), hot and red peppers (*all'arrabbiata* – rabid!) and *alla carbonara*, made with salt pork, eggs and cream.

Saltimbocca, the picturesque name meaning "jump in the mouth," is slices of ham on top of slices of veal, flavored with sage, fried in butter and then braised in white wine. *Straciatella* is another well known dish, a clear soup with a mixture of eggs, flour and cheese poured into it. It breaks up as it cooks, forming the "little rags" that give the soup its name.

For dessert you might be offered *zuppa inglese*, neither soup nor English, but a rich trifle flavored with rum.

The mountainous region of Umbria is the biggest producer – and hence consumer – of meat in the whole of Italy. There is plenty of game in the higher regions, sheep and goats a little further down and cattle and pigs on the foothills. The pork in particular is excellent. The animals are fattened on acorns and much of the meat is cured and turned into sausages spiced with garlic, pepper, pine nuts and fennel.

Umbria is famed even in France for its superb truffles, eaten sliced on pasta, and for its freshwater fish, in particular the roach.

Most of the inhabitants of The Marches live along the coast, and it follows that fish is the staple of their diet. Each seaside town has its own way of making fish soup, with the ingredients varying according to the day's catch. There are also snails flavored with fennel, and huge fat olives.

The Wines of Lazio

LAZIO

Lazio has two main wine producing areas: the Castelli Romani in the hills near Rome and the area around Lake Bolsena, about 96 km (60 miles) away.

CASTELLI ROMANI

This is an area of 129 sq km (50 sq miles) in the Alban hills producing mainly white wine that can be either sweet or dry. The grapes for the sweet wine are allowed to dry out a little on the vine before they are picked and fermented in the caves of the Alban hills. The sweet wines go well with fresh fruit and the dry wines complement robust Roman pasta dishes and their suckling pigs and lambs. The best known of these wines is Frascati, clear gold in color and either dry, semi-sweet or sweet.

CASTELBRACCIANO

A sweet, golden-yellow wine from the shores of Lake Bracciano.

CASTRENSE

Light red and white wines from the shores of Lake Bolsena.

CECUBO

A wine from Gaeta drunk by Cicero and Horace. It is a very light red with a full fragrance.

EST! EST!! EST!!!

There is a curious tale of how this wine came by its name. Local legend has it that an 18th century cardinal on a journey around Italy sent his steward before him to try out the wines in various hostelries. When the steward discovered a good one, he was to chalk Est! ("It is") on the door. At Montefiascone he was so impressed that he chalked Est! Est!! Est!!! before passing out to a stupor. The cardinal arrived and his enthusiasm for the wine was so great that he drank himself to death on it there and then.

The Wines of Umbria and The Marches

Wine production here is not extensive. The hillsides are very steep and in many cases vines are grown alternating with rows of corn. Both red and white are generally on the rough side, but there are two notable exceptions – Verdicchio dei Castelli di Jesi from The Marches, and Orvieto from Umbria.

ALTE VALLE DEL TENERE
The wines of the upper Tiber, both red and white, are light and simple and ideal for lunchtime drinking.

BIANCHELLO
A light dry white from The Marches, it goes well with fish.

ORVIETO
Made mainly from the Trebbiano grape, this wine has been produced around the cathedral city of Orvieto for at least 500 years. There are two straw-colored whites, one dry and the other semi-sweet. The grapes for the semi-sweet are allowed to begin to rot after they have been picked – in the German Auslese the grapes start to rot on the vine – and the resulting wine is not too sweet to be drunk with fish or poultry. The dry Orvieto is the more popular export.

VERDICCHIO DEI CASTELLI DI JESI
This wine is drunk along the holiday coast around Rimini and is also exported in large quantities. It is one of the very best of the Italian whites, despite the vulgar bottle. Straw-colored and slightly bitter, the best Verdicchio has a secondary fermentation like Chianti.

VIN COTTO
"Cooked wine" is made by reducing must over heat and then adding uncooked must. The wine is fermented and kept for two years. It is strong, rich and sweet.

Naples and The South

Naples is the gastronomic center of the south, just as Bologna is of the north, and it sets the tone of the cooking of Calabria, Basilicata, Apulia and Abruzzi-Molise, as well as its own region of Campania. Campania is the south's most fertile region and grows wheat, corn and millet as well as huge crops of all kinds of vegetables, especially tomatoes. All the ingredients are at hand for Naples' most celebrated and most exported dish, pizza. In Naples seafood is plentiful and a favorite spaghetti sauce is *con vongole*, with clams. Campania breeds the large white buffaloes whose milk is turned into mozzarella.

In the rest of the south, the land is mountainous, parched and poor. Olive oil rather than butter is the cooking medium – it costs less to keep an olive tree than a cow, and olive trees survive in poorer soil. Under the searing sun tempers run high, and the food is as fiery as those who eat it. Dried tubular pasta is served with angry sauces of garlic, hot peppers and burning chilies that take a little getting used to before their flavors can be truly appreciated.

The cooking of these poorer regions is largely based on pasta and vegetables, often cooked together in a substantial soup. Fish soups of all kinds are made around the coast, but transport is difficult through the rocky terrain and fish is not often available inland. Instead, the locals keep chickens that scratch about in the streets, and make imaginative use of their hens' eggs, even combining them with sheep's tripe in one dish.

The Wines of Naples and The South

CAMPANIA

Wine has been cultivated here since Roman times, but Campania is not a region renowned for its fine wines. Much of what it produces today is for blending, and a great deal of it, of course, supplies the local tourist trade.

AGLIANICO

A robust red from the grape of the same name, which is grown all over southern Italy.

CAPRI

Red, white and rosé wines come from the island, but there are also mainland wines bottled under the same name. The white is straw-yellow with a fresh taste and a hint of bitterness and highly thought of by the locals. All three are acceptable table wines made from a mixture of grapes.

COLLI SORRENTINI AND SORRENTO

Red, white and rosé wines, some of which appear as "Capri" or as "Sarriso di Sorrento," which particularly appeal to the more romantic tourist.

FALERNO

Both dry and sweet white and red wines come from the plain north of Naples. The white is straw-yellow with a hint of amber and a full flavor.

ISCHIA

Ischia Bianco is a delicate white, drunk young and chilled. It is made from a mixture of Biancolella and Fontana grapes. The reds from the island are not quite as individual, and some are rather coarse.

LACRIMA CHRIST

This is a very popular wine because of its memorable name (tears of Christ), but only the dry, German-style white lives up to its reputation. Other wines, including reds and rosés grown on the slopes of Vesuvius, are sold under this name and can be disappointing.

ABRUZZI-MOLISE

Craggy and mountainous, this region is not a great wine producer. What it does produce is either drunk locally or sent north for blending.

ABRUZZI BIANCO

A sharp, fresh white from the Trebbiano grape that makes a good accompaniment to fish.

ABRUZZI ROSSO

From the Montepulciano grape; it has a light tingle.

APULIA, BASILICATA AND CALABRIA

In the hot south of Italy, wine production is the main source of income – in fact Apulia produces more wine than any other region of Italy. But because of the heavy soil and the fierce sun, and the fact that the vines are grown close to the ground so that extra heat is reflected up at them, the wine tends to be coarse and strong. The reds are used for blending and the whites as a base for the vermouth industry in Turin.

ALEATICO

A rich, sweet dessert wine from the grape of the same name. The must is taken off the skins of part dried and fermentation is halted by the addition of spirits. The result is quite strong (14–17 percent).

CASTEL DEL MONTE

A fresh tingling white wine from the Bombino Bianco grape.

CASTELLANA

Red and rosé wines drunk very young and mainly used for blending.

LOCOROTONDO

Seeds and skin are removed from a mixture of grapes to produce a characterless white wine used mainly as a base for vermouth.

Sicily and Sardinia

Sicily and Sardinia owe a lot of the distinctiveness of their cooking to the invaders from Greece, Phoenicia and Spain who have occupied the islands over the centuries. Both subsist mainly on a diet of pasta and bread, but Sicily produces early vegetables, olives and citrus fruit as well as wheat, while Sardinia is a pastoral island almost entirely devoted to rearing sheep and, to a lesser extent, goats.

From the Saracens, Sicily learned the art of making delicious sweets and pastries, among them *cannoli*, filled with cream cheese, chocolate and candied fruit, and *cassata*, a layered cake that includes the same ingredients plus liqueur, and is sometimes covered in chocolate. Baking is a national pastime in Sicily. There are large loaves like cartwheels and savory rolls stuffed with pork, bacon and cheese.

Sardinians bake thin brittle circles of bread called *carta di musica*, music paper, and are fond of roasting whole sheep and goats, as well as wild boar, suckling pig and smaller game, on an outdoor spit. Instead of using herbs, they build their fires of aromatic woods, such as juniper or olive, to give the barbecued meat its distinctive flavor.

The island of Sardinia gave its name to the sardine, which swims in its waters along with lobsters and eels – and all these are cooked as simply as they were thousands of years ago.

The Wines of Sicily and Sardinia

Sardinia's inhabitants are unlike mainland Italians, being more somber and reserved. Their wines are just as individual, many of them being as strong as sherry. The whites are pinkish and the reds are so dark they are called *vini neri* – black wines.

Most of the wines of Sicily are strong and rough, and most are produced in large co-operatives and used for blending. The one major exception is Marsala, the distinctive dessert wine. The production of Marsala was set up around 1760 by a Liverpudlian, John Woodhouse, who visited the island and realized that the wine produced there resembled the base wines of port, sherry and Madeira. Marsala is drunk as a dessert wine or an aperitif. It is also blended with egg yolks to make the rich, creamy dessert called *zabaglione*.

The dry local white wine is fortified with wine brandy and sweetened with a local sweet, syrupy wine made with part-dried grapes and unfermented grape juice.

BASIC RECIPES

Pasta, gnocchi and pizza are probably the best known components of Italian cuisine. Their popularity ensures that they can be bought from most large supermarkets and some delicatessens – but nothing can quite compare with the taste of the genuine home-made article.

Basic Equipment

Knives are of the utmost importance to
the smooth functioning of an Italian kitchen.
(1) large, sharp chef's knife; (2) vegetable paring
knife; (4) fruit knife; (5) mezzaluna – a twin-handled,
double - bladed chopper; (6) cleaver;
(7) grapefruit knife.

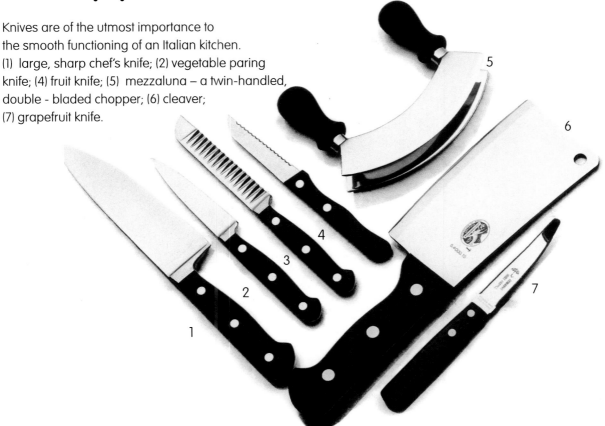

Many Italian kitchens now boast a hand-turned pasta
rolling and cutting machine. It ensures fine, even threads of
tagliatelle and thin, smooth sheets of lasagne.

A hand-held rotary cutter and a ravioli tray are very useful
for making meat, cheese or vegetable-filled pastas.

Top row, left to right:
1 wholewheat bucatini;
2 maccheroncini; 3 semolina spaghetti;
4 large macaroni; 5 wholewheat
spaghetti.

Second row, left to right:
6 creste; 7 sedanini; 8 lumachine;
9 elbow macaroni; 10 farfalle.

Third row:, left to right:
11 lumacone; 12 vegetable macaroni;
13 marille; 14 penne; 15 cannelloni.

Fourth row, left to right:
16 green bigoli; 17 long fusili; 18 viti;
19 green vitti; 20 refinelle; 21 trenitte.

Bottom row, left to right:
22 lasagne; 23 fettucini; 24 tagliatelle;
25 zite; 26 papardelle; 27 thin
papardelle or mafaldini.

Basic Ingredients

Pasta

A 450 g (1 lb) packet of dried pasta will serve five people. Bring 4 l (8 pt) water to the boil in a large saucepan. Add a pinch of salt and about 1 tsp oil. Add the pasta and increase the heat to get the water back to boiling point as quickly as possible. Cook it at a full rolling boil, stirring occasionally with a wooden spoon, for about 10 minutes.

Remember that pasta continues to cook for a few moments when you take it off the heat, so allow for this by stopping when the pasta is just *al dente*. When it is ready, add a cup or two of cold water to stop cooking and then drain. Meticulous draining is not necessary, as pasta should not dry out. (Italians say pasta is greedy for water). The process is exactly the same for fresh pasta, but you will need about 225 g (8 oz) pasta per person, and the cooking time will be only about 4 minutes.

Taste in pasta divides Italy roughly in two. In the north of Italy and as far south as Rome, the pasta is mainly of the ribbon variety – flat, fresh and homemade with egg. Around Naples and further south it is tubular, eggless, mass-produced and dried.

Pasta for soups includes conchigliette (little shells), anellini (little hoops), nocchette (little bows) and semini (little seeds).

Pasta to be boiled includes fettucine (ribbons), fusilli (spirals), spaghetti, ziti (fat spaghetti), conchiglie (shells), penne (nibs), cappelletti (hats), farfalle (bows), macaroni and ruote (wheels).

Pasta to be stuffed includes lumache (snails), cannelloni, ravioli and tortellini.

Herbs

There is no doubt that fresh herbs have much to add to the flavors we create in the kitchen. As it is possible to buy potted herbs from garden centers and packets of fresh herbs from many supermarkets and vegetable shops, it is worth the effort to cook with fresh herbs.

Many of the herbs so characteristic of Italian cooking were originally used by the Romans medicinally as well as in cooking. With the increasing interest in fresh food and healthy diets, most people are also more aware of the value and taste of fresh herbs. It is worth cultivating your own as they are decorative and edible. Many urban gardeners grow their own herbs very successfully, even on windowsills and balconies, and it is certainly interesting to try. Here are a few that grow in town most successfully and which are indispensable in pasta and pizza cooking. Dried herbs are inevitably necessary at certain times of the year and they make quite acceptable substitutes; it is best to buy them in small quantities as and when you need them. A jar of dried herbs that has been in the cupboard for over a year will not have much flavor remaining.

BASIL

A wonderful aromatic herb, basil is an excellent herb for flavoring tomato sauces, and an essential ingredient in authentic Genoese pesto. Basil plants need the sun and a warm sheltered position. Pinching the tops of the plants will encourage the plant to bush and prevent flowers growing. If you move it to the kitchen windowsill in winter, you should manage to keep a small supply of fresh basil going for a couple of months.

BAY

Bay trees are ideal for balconies and patios. The tree should be kept in a sheltered position in winter. When removing leaves for culinary use, take care not to spoil the shape. The occasional clipping of branches and constant picking of leaves will usually remove the need for heavy pruning. Bay is an essential ingredient in bouquet garni.

BOUQUET GARNI

This is a small bunch of fresh or dried herbs that are tied together with a piece of string.

Place dried herbs in a small muslin bag. There are now many different commercially prepared bouquet garni sachets, which are good substitutes if fresh herbs are not available.

To make fresh bouquet garni, take one bay leaf, a good sprig of thyme and two stalks of parsley and tie together using string or thick thread.

CHIVES
This spiky herb belonging to the onion family is excellent for flavoring sauces and dressings. It grows well in pots It freezes well for use in the winter.

CILANTRO
This distinctive plant with dark green glossy leaves is a hardy southern European herb. It is used extensively in Oriental cooking and is good for flavoring vegetable dishes as well as making a pretty garnish. Cilantro can be grown in pots or tubs.

DILL
This is another pretty culinary herb that can be grown in tubs or pots. Fresh dill goes particularly well with many fish dishes and sauces. The long feathery fronds also make a pretty garnish.

MARJORAM/OREGANO
The decorative wild marjoram is also easily grown in small containers and is suitable for flavoring sauces to accompany pasta. Its flavor is not quite as strong as that of the Mediterranean variety, oregano.

MINT
The many varieties of mint all have slightly different flavors. Experiment with two or three different mints until you find the one you like best. The leaves are widely used in cooking. Mint leaves add taste and body to pasta salads and are also an attractive garnish. Two of the most popular varieties are applemint and spearmint.

PARSLEY
Many varieties of parsley can be grown in large pots and tubs. Parsley can be used in quite large quantities and therefore it is cheaper to grow it from seed than to buy whole plants.

ROSEMARY
This plant was brought to Western world by the Romans. It must be planted in a sheltered position to survive the winter in colder climates. Rosemary is a pretty, spiky bush and its aromatic leaves are a must for cooking, especially in lamb and vegetable dishes.

SAGE
A distinctive plant with silvery leaves, which has the advantage of being fairly hardy once it is established. The leaves are particularly popular in savory stuffings. This herb should be grown in a large pot and left for a year before being robbed of too many leaves.

THYME
This is yet another plant that comes from the Mediterranean region. There are several pretty varieties that can be grown in pots and they all provide flavorings for many of the classic sauces that accompany pasta. The little spiky leaves are evergreen and can be picked and used even in the winter.

DRYING HERBS
Dry herbs in a dark, warm atmosphere, a low oven at approximately 38°C/100°F/Gas Mark ¼. Air must circulate freely around the herbs.

FREEZING HERBS
The rule for freezing is that only leafy herbs such as parsley, chervil, coriander and sage retain their color and flavor really well. Small packets of frozen herbs can easily be crumbled into sauces during cooking. The spiky leaves of thyme and rosemary are probably better dried.

Some fresh herbs can be frozen in ice cube trays. Mint cubes, for example, are delicious in summer drinks.

Egg Pasta

Serves 4
400 g (14 oz) all-purpose flour
4 medium eggs
vegetable oil

1 Dust a board or work surface with flour. Mound the flour onto the board and make a well in the center.

2 Break the eggs into the well and beat with a fork.

3 Gradually work in the flour. When the dough stiffens, use your hands.

4 Knead vigorously for at least 10 minutes.

5 When bubbles appear, roll the dough into a ball and then flatten it.

Using a Pasta Machine
The dough should be firmer than for hand-rolled pasta. Feed dough into the machine in small pieces, each rolled in flour, so it will not be as likely to stick to the blades.

6 Roll out with a rolling pin. Starting from the center, roll out in all directions.

7 Turn the dough around, using a rolling pin.

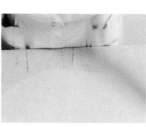

8 Put it back down on the board and continue to roll out in the other direction.

Red Pasta

Serves 4
225 g (8 oz) carrots
1 tsp tomato paste
200 g (7 oz) all-purpose flour
3 eggs
pinch of salt

1 The amount of flour used here will vary according to the moisture content of the carrots. Peel and steam the carrots and press through a fine strainer into a saucepan. Put the saucepan over heat and stir with a wooden spoon to dry out the purée. Stir in the tomato paste and let it cool.
2 Proceed as for egg pasta (see page 34), adding the carrot mixture to the eggs in the flour well. Add more flour if necessary. This pasta, like the green variety below, does not roll out as thinly as basic pasta dough.

Green Pasta

Serves 4
100 g (4 oz) very well drained, cooked spinach
200 g (7 oz) all-purpose flour
3 eggs

1 Press the spinach through a strainer or purée in a blender.
2 Make the pasta dough (see page 34), add the spinach and knead for 10 minutes. If the dough is too soft, add a little more flour. It is difficult to roll out pasta very thinly.

Tagliatelle

Tagliatelle is the simplest pasta shape to make – therefore it is probably the most commonly found. Make the pasta – white, red or green – (see recipes above or opposite). Roll out as thinly as possible, then, beginning at one end, roll the dough into a long, thin cylinder. Beginning at one end, cut the roll into slices. When the roll has been cut into slices, gently ease the slices into separate strands of tagliatelle.

1 Using a knife with a wide blade, cut the roll into slices of the desired thickness.

2 Separate and spread out the pieces of tagliatelle on the board.

Cappelletti

1 Prepare the pasta as for tagliatelle (see page 35), and let it rest under a cloth. Using a little serrated cutter or a sharp knife, cut the pasta into squares with 2.5–4 cm (1–1½ in) long sides.

2 Place a pea-sized amount of filling in the middle of each square, then fold into a triangle.

3 Keeping your left index finger under the filling, join the two points of the triangle, making sure that there is no hole. Stretch sideways a little, if necessary.

Cappelletti Toscani

1 Prepare the egg pasta dough (see page 34) with 3 eggs to 400 g (14 oz) flour and cut out circles.

2 Cut out circles on rolled-out dough, place meat filling on top, and fold in half.

3 Press the edges round the filling, then join the two points of the half-moon shape. There should be a small hole in the center.

Tortellini and Tortelloni

1. Prepare the green pasta (see page 35) and roll out into a sheet. Cover the pasta with a cloth to avoid drying out.
2. Using a little serrated cutter or a sharp knife, cut the pasta into squares with 2.5–4 cm (1–1½ in) long sides.

Filling the Tortellini

3. Place a nut-sized piece of filling – either meat or ricotta and spinach – towards one corner of a square of pasta.

4. Fold the top over to form a triangle and join the points together to make a curved shape.

Making Tortellini Gratin

5. Place the tortelloni in a shallow dish and cover with Tomato Sauce (see page 88).

6. Cover with a thick layer of mozzarella cheese. Cook for 45 minutes or until bubbling, then serve.

Agnolini

1. Prepare the pasta as for tagliatelle (see page 35), making the dough a little firmer, as it is to be rolled out more thinly.

Making the Agnolini

2. Cut the pasta into strips 2.5 cm (1 in) wide and place the strips on top of one another.

3. Using a sharp knife, cut the strips into squares.

4. Put filling in the center of each square and fold the pasta over.

5. Put your index finger against the side where the pasta was folded and turn the two ends around your finger.

Ravioli

1 Prepare the pasta as for tagliatelle (see page 35), do not rest the dough. Roll the dough and mark with a pastry wheel into 2.5 cm (1 in) squares.
2 Place the stuffing in the squares and top with another strip of rolled out pasta. Cut around the squares with the wheel and place on a flat tray.

These filled pasta squares are common to all parts of Italy. They can be made with plain or egg pasta and are like tortellini (see page 38). Make them square or round. To make ravioli in the traditional fashion, roll pasta into a sheet, dot with filling, and then top with a second sheet.

Polenta

Polenta can be made either from finely ground cornmeal, coarser cornmeal or from buckwheat flour.

To cook polenta follow you will need to use the following proportions: 210 g (7½ oz) cornmeal to 1.5 l (3 pt) salted water, and this should not come more than halfway up the saucepan. The quantities vary according to how it is to be served. If a sauce is to be served with it, for four people you will need 500 g (1 lb 2 oz) cornmeal and 2.5 l (5 pt) water. For coarse meal, boil the water, then add the meal gradually in handfuls, stirring to avoid lumps.

The cooking time will vary from 40 minutes to about an hour. Stir the mixture constantly, scraping the sides and bottom. When the polenta comes away easily from the sides of the saucepan at the end of the cooking time, loosen it from the saucepan with a slotted spoon moistened in cold water and pour out. Serve the polenta very hot, or spread into a dough to be used for gnocchi or other pasta dishes..

If you use finer polenta, add a fifth of it to the cold water before putting it onto boil, then cover the saucepan and bring to a boil. Boil for 10 minutes, then gradually add the rest and proceed as above.

Potato Gnocchi

Serves 4
450 g (1 lb) russet potatoes
1 tsp salt
2 eggs
150 g (5 oz) all-purpose flour

Preparing Gnocchi (see step by step images below left)

1 Peel the potatoes and boil them in salted water over low heat. Use even-sized potatoes, so that they cook evenly. When just tender, drain, and mash while still hot and put onto a board.

2 Make a well in the middle of the mashed potatoes and put in the salt and eggs. Then pour on the flour and mix well to give a firm dough that does not stick to your hands. The amount of flour will vary depending on how moist the potatoes are Knead the dough for a few minutes.

3 Cut off a piece of dough and roll into a cylinder on the floured board.

4 Cut off 2.5 cm (1 in) slices, roll into balls and flour well. Take a grater (or fork) and decorate the gnocchi with holes or ridges, pressing in with your finger on one side to give a shell shape.

1

2

3

4

Cook's Tip
To cook the gnocchi, bring a large saucepan of salted water to the boil and put all the gnocchi into the pan. Continue to boil the water, when the gnocchi float to the surface they are cooked.

Semolina Gnocchi

Serves 4

900 ml (2 pt) milk
salt
120 g (4½ oz) fine
    semolina
100 g (4 oz) butter
6 tsp Parmesan
    cheese

2 egg yolks
black pepper
pinch of ground
    nutmeg
breadcrumbs

1 Heat the milk with a pinch of salt, and when it boils gradually add the semolina, stirring the whole time with a wooden spoon to avoid lumps. Cook, stirring, for 20 minutes.

2 Remove from the heat and add 2 tbsp butter in small pieces. Then gradually stir in 2 tbsp Parmesan cheese, the egg yolks, one at a time, a pinch of pepper and nutmeg.

3 Oil one or two large dishes or a clean marble kitchen slab and pour the mixture on.

4 Spread out to 1 cm (½ in) thickness using a cold wet spatula and leave to cool.

5 Preheat the oven to 180°C/350°F/Gas Mark 4. Melt the remaining butter; use some of the butter to grease a casserole. Cut out squares or circles of semolina dough to create the gnocchi, and place in the greased dish. Drizzle with butter and sprinkle with Parmesan, add a second layer of gnocchi, and so on. Sprinkle the breadcrumbs over the gnocchi and bake for about 20 minutes or until golden brown.

1

2

3

4

Pizza Dough

Serves 4
25 g (1 oz) fresh yeast
   or 1 packet active dried yeast
100 g (4 oz) all-purpose flour
pinch of salt

1   Crumble the yeast into a cup and dissolve in about
    4 tbsp lukewarm water (35°C/95°F). For dry yeast,
    use warm water (45°C/110°F). Mix in about 25 g
    (1 oz) of flour, cover the cup with a cloth and
    leave in a warm place to rise. Put the remaining
    flour into a bowl, add a pinch of salt.

2   Put the yeast mixture in a well in the middle of
    the bowl of flour.

3   Work in the yeast mixture gradually using a
    palette knife or spatula, mix until you have a firm,
    elastic dough, adding just enough water. Work in
    carefully to avoid the dough becoming sticky.

4   Turn the dough out onto a floured board and
    knead for 10 minutes, then roll the dough into a
    ball.

5   Place the dough in a lightly floured bowl, and
    cover with plastic wrap. Leave to rise in a warm
    place until the dough has doubled in size.

6   Turn the risen dough onto a floured board. Knead
    and knock back (punch down) until all air pockets
    are eliminated. The dough should be smooth, firm
    and elastic.

4

5

6

ANTIPASTI

...sti are savory morsels designed to whet the appetite. Serve an ...ctive arrangement of eggs, olives, pickled vegetables, artichoke hearts, ...sparagus and anchovies, or paper-thin slices of prosciutto with melon or ...figs, or choose from any of the following recipes.

Roast Vegetables in Oil

Serves 2–4
2 peppers (red, yellow or green)
1 eggplant
4 zucchini
150 ml (5 fl oz) olive oil
salt and freshly ground black pepper

1 Preheat the oven to 190°C/370°F/Gas Mark 5. Halve the peppers and seed them. Cut off the coarse stem of the eggplant and trim the zucchini.
2 Lay the peppers and eggplant directly onto the oven shelves. Do not baste them. Cook for 10 minutes, then add the zucchini.
3 Remove all the vegetables after 15 minutes' cooking, when they will be soft.
4 Slice the peppers and eggplant, and cut the zucchini in half lengthways.
5 Layout the vegetables in a ovenproof dish, brush with the oil and season to taste. Pour over what remains of the oil and roast in the oven for a further 20 minutes and serve hot, cold or at room temperature.

Cook's Tip
The vegetables roast in their own juices and thus intensify their own natural goodness. Basta!

Baked Stuffed Tomatoes

Serves 4
8 large ripe tomatoes
1 onion, finely chopped
vegetable oil
8 anchovy fillets, rinsed, pounded into a paste
1 bunch parsley, chopped
3 tbsp capers
2 tbsp breadcrumbs
25 g (1 oz) sliced olives
salt and freshly ground black pepper
ground nutmeg (optional)

1 Preheat the oven to 175°C/350°F/Gas Mark 4. Cut a lid from the top of each tomato and reserve. Scoop out some of the flesh, seed, chop and set aside. Turn the tomatoes over to drain.
2 Fry the onion in a little oil; add the chopped tomatoes, anchovies, parsley, capers, breadcrumbs and olives. Season with salt, pepper and a little nutmeg, if desired, and mix well. Divide the stuffing between the tomatoes. Top each with the reserved top slice.
3 Put the tomatoes in a baking dish, drizzle oil over them and bake for 30 minutes.

Asparagus with Parmesan and Fried Eggs

Serves 4
1 kg (2 lb) fresh asparagus
salt to taste
75 g (3 oz) butter
50 g (2 oz) freshly grated Parmesan cheese
4 eggs
2 tbsp olive oil

1 Preheat the oven to 190°C/375°F/Gas Mark 5. Trim the coarse whitish ends from the asparagus spears.

2 Boil the asparagus in salted water for about 10 minutes. (If you can keep the heads above the surface of the water, so much the better. Steamed, they have a better chance of remaining intact).

3 Grease the bottom of a flat, ovenproof dish with one third of the butter. It should be large enough to accommodate the asparagus in two layers.

4 When the asparagus has cooked, arrange it in the dish.

5 Sprinkle the Parmesan over the asparagus and dot it with the remaining butter then bake until the cheese and butter form a light brown crust – about 10 minutes. In the meantime, fry the eggs carefully in the olive oil. You must not break the yolks.

6 To eat, dip the asparagus into the egg yolk.

Bruschetta with Tomato and Basil

Serves 6
6 slices thickly cut white bread, preferably Italian
450 g (1 lb) fresh tomatoes
50 g (2 oz) fresh basil
150 ml (5 fl oz) olive oil
salt and freshly ground black pepper

1. In a low oven, toast the bread until each slice is completely dry and crisp.
2. Roughly dice the tomatoes (there is no need to peel them), and finely chop the basil.
3. Mix the basil, olive oil and seasoning with the tomatoes.
4. Spoon on top of the bread slices and serve immediately. (The bread should still be slightly warm).

Grilled Mussels

Serves 4–6
1 kg (2 lb) fresh mussels
100 g (4 oz) fresh breadcrumbs
50 g (2 oz) freshly grated Parmesan cheese
4 tbsp parsley, finely chopped
4 large cloves garlic, finely chopped
salt and freshly ground black pepper
150 ml (5 fl oz) olive oil

1. Preheat the oven to 200°C/400°F/Gas Mark 6. Thoroughly scrub the mussels, removing all beards and barnacles.
2. Place a saucepan of water large enough to hold them all on low heat, add the mussels and cover. Cook for about 5 minutes.
3. In the meantime, combine the breadcrumbs, Parmesan, parsley, garlic, salt and pepper in a bowl.
4. Take the mussels off the heat, drain and set the cooking liquid aside.
5. Remove the top shell from each mussel, leaving the flesh in the lower shell. Discard any mussels that have failed to open. Lay the half-shell mussels on a baking tray and sprinkle the breadcrumb mixture into each shell.
6. Combine the oil and the reserved mussel liquid and pour a little onto each mussel. Return the stuffed mussels to a hot broiler, or the preheated oven, and bake for 3–4 minutes.

Beef Carpaccio

Serves 4

300 ml (10 fl oz) olive oil
4 large cloves garlic
4 anchovy fillets
1 red whole chili, diced
capers
450 g (1 lb) fillet mignon
salt and freshly ground black pepper to taste
juice of 2 lemons

1. Heat the oil over low heat until it is hot, but not hot enough to fry.
2. Add the garlic, anchovy fillets and the chili and let them stew in the oil for 20 minutes. (On no account should there be any sizzle. You are not frying these ingredients but letting their flavors soak into the oil).
3. While the marinade is cooking, slice the beef as finely as you can. You will need to use a very sharp knife or a mandolin. There is no such thing as too fine. Lay the slices out on a flat dish, lightly salt them, add pepper to taste and pour over the lemon juice.
4. Remove the oil from the heat after 20 minutes. Allow it to cool then pour it over the beef.
5. Chill the dish for 12 hours. Before serving, remove the garlic and any intact pieces of anchovy. Best served with capers, rocket and Parmesan.

Parmesan Cheese Fritters

Serves 4

100 g (4 oz) fresh Parmesan cheese in one piece
400 g (14 oz) all-purpose flour
pinch of baking powder
salt
175 g (6 oz) butter or solid margarine, slightly
    softened and diced
vegetable oil or solid margarine

1 Cut the Parmesan into thin slivers, or grate coarsely. Pour the flour, baking powder and 1 tbsp salt onto a board. Make a well in the center and add 75 g (3 oz) butter or margarine. Rub well into the flour and add enough lukewarm water to form into a dough. Knead for 10 minutes and then roll out into a thin rectangular sheet.

2 Arrange little heaps of cheese at intervals in a row 5 cm (2 in) from edge of pastry. Dot piles of cheese with remaining 2 tbsp butter or margarine. Fold pastry over cheese and press down well with your fingers.

3 With a pastry cutter or a knife, cut off filled strip and cut around each mound of cheese, making sure the edges are well sealed into squares or oblongs.

4 Fry filled pastries in plenty of hot oil or margarine. Remove when golden brown and puffed up and drain on paper towels. Arrange on a serving dish, garnish with parsley and serve very hot.

Parmesan

Parmesan is the best known of all Italian cheeses. It accompanies pasta and rice and is ideal for cooking as it does not turn stringy as it melts. It is also delicious at the end of a meal with fruit. If you can avoid it, never buy pre-grated Parmesan sold in cartons – it has no taste. Parmesan bought by the chunk should be pale yellow and finely honeycombed – the generic name for this cheese in Italy is *grana*, referring to its fine grain. The best *grana* is four years old and correspondingly expensive. Store large pieces of Parmesan wrapped in two or three sheets of foil at the bottom of the fridge.

Mozzarella in Carriages

Serves 4
10 slices square white bread, crusts trimmed
thinly sliced mozzarella cheese
all-purpose flour
2 eggs
1–2 tbsp whipping cream or milk
salt
vegetable oil or butter

1 Cover half the bread slices with cheese. Press the remaining bread on top. Pour cold water into a bowl and put a little flour into a second bowl. Dip each sandwich first in the flour, then water, holding the edges firmly, and arrange on the bottom of a large dish.
2 Break the eggs into a cup, beat with the cream or milk and a pinch of salt, and pour over the sandwiches. Turn the sandwiches over to coat completely with egg mixture. Leave to stand for 10 minutes.
3 Heat some oil or butter in a frying pan and brown the sandwiches on both sides. Serve very hot.

Sardines with Pepper and Tomato Sauce

Serves 4
12 sardines in oil
1 green or red pepper, roasted, skinned and cut into strips
whites of 3 hard boiled eggs, chopped
275 g (10 oz) peeled, seeded, chopped tomatoes
2 tbsp butter
few fresh sage leaves, chopped
1 clove garlic, crushed
salt and pepper

1 Bone the sardines carefully and reassemble them on a serving dish. Decorate with the pepper and egg whites. Press the tomatoes through a strainer and cream with the butter, sage and garlic. Season with salt and pepper and spoon over the sardines.

Sardines
Sardines are known by many different names in Italy. The Italians say the sardine has 24 virtues and loses one every hour – therefore it should be eaten very fresh. To prepare fresh sardines, slit open the stomach and pull out the entrails and backbone. Cut off the head, if preferred. Fresh sardines are delicious grilled over an open fire with a little rosemary, black pepper and lemon juice or dipped in flour, egg and breadcrumbs and fried.

SOUPS

Soup is rarely served in Italy at the same meal as pasta, as it often contains pasta itself. An Italian soup may be a delicate consommé garnished with dumplings or eggs, or it may be a nourishing broth thickened with rice and vegetables. Offer Parmesan cheese with anything other than a fish soup.

Pastine in Brodo

Serves 4–6
1 medium onion
1 large carrot
2 sticks celery
1 small fennel bulb
½ medium fresh green pepper
1 medium potato
1 ripe fresh tomato (about 100 g (4oz))
1 kg (2 lb) assorted meat off cuts and bones
225 g (8 oz) dried pasta stars
salt

1 Put all the ingredients except the pasta and the salt into 1.5 l (3 pt) cold water.
2 Bring the liquid very slowly to just under a boil and hold it there. (Boiling makes stock cloudy). Cook for 3 hours. Skim the broth constantly, or, when it is cooked, allow to cool and then lift off the solidified fats. (This will considerably lengthen the preparation process).
3 When the broth is cooked and skimmed, add the pasta. Since you have carefully removed all the fats, you may now boil it. Do so for about 10 minutes, or until the pasta shells are just soft. Season with salt and serve.

Country Chickpea Soup

Serves 4
450 g (1 lb) dried chickpeas
50 g (2 oz) chopped pancetta
1 scallion, chopped
1 clove garlic, sliced
1 tbsp parsley, chopped
pinch of dried leaf marjoram
2 tbsp vegetable oil
150 g (5 oz) peeled, chopped tomatoes
175 g (6 oz) chopped lean pork
salt and pepper
4 slices toast
75 g (3 oz) Parmesan cheese, grated

1 Soak the chickpeas in lukewarm water for 12 hours. Put the pancetta, scallion, garlic, parsley and marjoram into a saucepan. Stir in oil, drained chickpeas and tomatoes; add enough water to cover. Bring to a boil.
2 Add the pork, reduce heat to medium, cover and simmer for 2 hours. Season with salt and a pinch of pepper and mix. Lay slices of toast in the bottom of four soup bowls and pour the soup on. Sprinkle with Parmesan.

Chickpeas
Chickpeas are often served in Italy with pasta (in a dish called *tuoni e lampo* – thunder and lighting) or in soups. The dried ones should be soaked for 12 hours and simmered for 2–6 hours until tender. As this is a lengthy process, it may be easier to buy the canned variety.

Bean Soup with Parsley, Garlic and Chili

Serves 4

350 g (12 oz) dried white kidney beans
4 cloves garlic
4 tbsp olive oil
4 tbsp tomato paste
2 tbsp finely fresh parsley, chopped
25 g (1 oz) fresh chilies
salt and freshly ground black pepper

1. Soak the kidney beans in double their volume of water overnight. Leave the saucepan near a low heat source, a radiator or pilot light, if you can.

2. A minimum of 1½ hours before you wish to serve the soup, drain the beans, cover them with more water and set them to boil over low heat. Cook them for between 40 and 60 minutes, until they are tender. If you are using them immediately, let them stand in their cooking water. Otherwise, drain and store covered in the fridge.

3. Peel and crush the garlic and soften it in the olive oil over low heat. As it begins to color, drain away as much of the oil as you can and set it aside.

4. Add the cooked beans, the tomato paste, the parsley and no more than 300 ml (10 fl oz) of water. Bring the mixture to a boil then lower the heat to simmer.

5. As the soup is cooking, slice and de-seed the fresh chilies and stew them very gently in the garlic-flavored olive oil until they are very soft. Pour the chili oil into a small serving bowl.

6. Take half the quantity of the bean soup and purée it. When the consistency is completely smooth, combine the two parts of the soup and season to taste.

Minestrone

Serves 6–8
50 g (2 oz) butter
4 tbsp olive oil
3 large onions
2 cloves garlic
225 g (8 oz) potatoes
225 g (8 oz) carrots
2 sticks celery
225 g (8 oz) cooked white kidney beans
100 g (4 oz) green beans
100 g (4 oz) zucchini
3 beef stock cubes or 1.5 l (3 pt) Pastine in
   Brodo (see page 52)
100 g (4 oz) chopped fresh or
   canned Italian tomatoes
100 g (4 oz) piece of Parmesan cheese rind
salt and freshly ground black pepper

1 Melt the butter and oil over medium heat. Finely chop the onions, garlic, potatoes, carrots and celery and add them, one vegetable at a time, to the oil and butter in a large saucepan. Cook each for 2–3 minutes, without browning.

2 Stir in the white and green beans. Chop the zucchini into large pieces and add them to the mixture.

3 Crumble in the stock cubes and stir in 1.4 l (3 pt) water. Stir in the chopped tomatoes and add the whole cheese rind.

4 Cook the whole mixture together until you have a substantially thick soup. Add water to maintain the desired consistency, if necessary, until the soup is thoroughly cooked – about 20 minutes. Season before serving and remember to remove the piece of cheese rind.

Cook's Tip
There are many versions of minestrone. Sometimes they contain pasta, sometimes rice and sometimes the mixture is thick with legumes. There are just two important rules: use a lot of vegetables and don't forget the cheese rind.

Minestrone, Livorno Style

Serves 4

450 g (1 lb) unshelled fresh broad beans
2 tbsp parsley, chopped
1 slice prosciutto
1 clove garlic
olive oil
½ small head savoy cabbage, grated
25 g (1 oz) trimmed, washed, grated spinach
1 onion, chopped
500 g (1¼ lb) potatoes, peeled, and chopped
100 g (4 oz) chopped carrot
1 stick celery, chopped
1 zucchini, chopped
1 stock cube
350 g (12 oz) peeled, seeded, chopped
   ripe tomatoes
100 g (4 oz) salt pork, blanched, cut into strips
salt
150 g (5 oz) rice
5 tbsp grated Parmesan cheese

1 In winter this can be prepared with dried soaked beans and tinned tomatoes. Shell the beans and put them into cold water.

2 Finely chop parsley, together with prosciutto and garlic. Put this in a frying pan with 3 tbsp oil. Cook for a few minutes, then add cabbage and spinach, stir and continue to cook over medium heat.

3 Add onion, potatoes, carrot, celery and courgettes. Pour in 1¼ l water, add stock cube, tomatoes and salt pork. When the water comes to a boil, add drained beans, cover and simmer gently for 2 hours. Season to taste with salt, add rice, stir and cook, uncovered, until rice is done. The soup should be thick. Remove from heat and stir in 2 tbsp Parmesan. Serve remaining Parmesan separately.

Minestrone with Pesto

Serves 4

225 g (8 oz) fresh spinach
175 g (6 oz) green beans
2 potatoes, peeled, sliced
½ head green cabbage, chopped
1 leek, sliced
½ onion, sliced
100g (4 oz) cherry tomatoes, skinned
2 tbsp vegetable oil
salt and freshly ground black pepper
1 tbsp Genoese Pesto (see page 83)
175 g (6 oz) rice
freshly grated Parmesan cheese
red basil leaves (optional)

1 Wash, trim and chop the spinach. Put in a saucepan with the beans, potatoes, cabbage, leek, tomatoes and onion. Stir in oil to coat. Season with salt and pepper and add 1.5 litres (3 pt) water.

2 Bring to a boil and cook over medium heat for 1 hour. Stir in the pesto, pour in the rice and cook for 15 more minutes. Serve in separate bowls, sprinkle with freshly grated Parmesan cheese.

3 Garnish with red basil leave, if desired.

Radicchio and Rice Soup with Fresh Sage

Serves 4
3 tbsp olive oil
1 small onion
2 cloves garlic
1 large head radicchio
900 ml (2 pt) Pastine in Brodo (see page 52), or 1 chicken stock cube
8 tbsp/100 g (4 oz) Arborio (risotto) rice
1 heaped tbsp freshly grated Parmesan cheese
5 tbsp fresh finely chopped sage – nothing else will do
salt and freshly ground black pepper

1   Heat the olive oil over medium heat. Finely slice the onion and sauté it until it softens. It must not color. Add the garlic, unchopped.
2   As the garlic and onions stew together, finely shred the radicchio. Add it to the saucepan and cook it until it softens completely – about 3–4 minutes.
3   Add the pastine in brodo, or crumble in the stock cube and add 900 ml (2 pt) water. Add the rice and cook everything together until the rice is cooked but still firm – *al dente.*
4   Whisk in the Parmesan and the finely chopped sage. Cook for another minute or so. Season and serve.

Radicchio
A speciality of Treviso, radicchio is shaped like a small round lettuce, but is rose-colored with cream veins. Radicchio from Castelfranco has darker streaks against a lighter ground. Purists say the two should never be mixed.

Potato and Onion Soup

Serves 4–6
4 tbsp butter
2 tbsp olive oil
675 g (1½ lb) onions
1 kg (2 lb) potatoes
Pastine in Brodo (see page 52 or 1½ beef stock cubes in 900 ml (2 pt) water
3 tbsp freshly grated Parmesan cheese
salt and freshly ground black pepper

1   Melt the oil and butter together over high heat. Finely chop the onions and cook them in the oil and butter until they turn light brown. Remove the saucepan from the heat.
2   Peel and dice the potatoes and boil them with the pastine in brodo or stock cubes until they are quite soft.
3   Now pour the potatoes and their water into the onion saucepan – which still contains the onions – and cook together for 10 more minutes. As the mixture cooks, press the potatoes into the sides of the saucepan to loosen any caramelized onion residue.
4   Stir the cheese into the soup, season and serve.

Lentil Soup

Serves 4–6

2 tbsp olive oil
1 medium onion
1 stick celery
25g (½ oz) dill
2 slices bacon or pancetta
225 g (8 oz) fresh or canned tomatoes
225 g (8 oz) brown or green lentils
Pastine in Brodo (see page 52), or 1 beef stock cube
    in 1.4 l (3 pt) water
salt and freshly ground black pepper
3 tbsp freshly grated Parmesan cheese
1 tbsp butter

1 In a large saucepan, heat the olive oil over medium heat.

2 Very finely slice the onion and soften it in the oil. Finely slice the celery and add it to the onion when it is soft. Cook for 2 more minutes or so.

3 As the celery is cooking, dice the bacon. Add it to the mixture and chop in the dill. Roughly chop the tomatoes and add them to the soup, together with the lentils.

4 Add the pastine in brodo or beef stock. Bring to a boil on high heat and then reduce to a simmer. You must cook the soup until the lentils are tender, up to 45 minutes. Test by tasting the soup occasionally. When the lentils are soft, season with the salt.

5 Off the heat, whisk in the butter and Parmesan. Pour the mixture into a suitable tureen, and generously coat the top with fresh black pepper. Garnish with a sprig of dill and serve with lemon.

Rice and Turnip Soup

Serves 4
2 tbsp parsley sprigs
2 strips bacon or pancetta
butter
2 medium turnips, peeled, thinly sliced
1.25 litres (2½ pt) beef stock
150 g (5 oz) rice
6 tbsp freshly grated Parmesan cheese

1 Finely chop the parsley together with the bacon. Fry for a few minutes in a little butter. Then add turnips and cook for a few minutes. Add stock, bring to a boil and simmer for 7 minutes. Add the rice, stir and cook, uncovered, until just *al dente*. If turnips are very young and tender you can add them when you put in the rice.

2 A minute before removing from heat, stir in 2 tbsp Parmesan, then serve, passing remaining cheese for people to serve themselves.

Salami and Pancetta

Each region of Italy has its own special kind of salami. Sometimes the meat is finely ground, giving a smooth texture and a pale pink color, or it may be coarse-ground so that the sausage has large chunks of dark red and white meat, often dotted with black peppercorns.

Pancetta is the same cut of pork as bacon, but cured in salt and spices instead of being smoked. It is rolled into a sausage shape and sold sliced.

Egg Pasta and Pea Soup

Serves 4
½ carrot, chopped
½ onion, chopped
½ stick celery, chopped
1 tbsp parsley, chopped
2 tbsp butter
1 tbsp tomato paste
salt and freshly ground black pepper
175 g (6 oz) shelled young, fresh peas
50 g (2 oz) small egg pasta shapes
50 g (2 oz) grated Parmesan cheese

1 Gently fry carrot, onion, celery and parsley in a saucepan with butter until golden brown. Add tomato paste diluted with 2 tbsp water, season with salt and pepper and cook for 10 minutes. Pour in 1.5 l (3 pt) water, bring to a boil and add peas. Cook for 25 minutes, add pasta and cook for 15 more minutes. Serve at once, passing remaining cheese for people to serve themselves.

Mussel and Potato Soup

Serves 4
700 g (1½ lb) mussels
vegetable oil
freshly ground black pepper
2 strips bacon
½ small onion
1 clove garlic
275 g (10 oz) peeled, sliced potatoes
salt
150 g (5 oz) rice

1   Pull off and discard the beards from the mussels, and rinse them well under cold running water. Cook in a large saucepan over low heat with a little oil and a pinch of freshly ground pepper until they open. Drain, reserving liquid, and discard any mussels that remain closed. Remove the mussels from their shells.
2   Chop the bacon, onion and garlic finely together and put into a saucepan with 1 tbsp oil. Pour in 1.2 l (2½ pt) water, add potatoes, season with salt and bring to a boil. Simmer for 10 minutes, then add the rice and cook briskly.
3   Just before the soup is cooked, strain the reserved mussel cooking liquid and add to the soup with the mussels. Heat through for a couple of minutes and serve.

Poached Egg in Broth

Serves 6
Pastine in Brodo (see page 52) or 1.4 l
   (3 pt) light broth
6 slices good Italian bread
6 eggs
3 tbsp freshly grated Parmesan
salt and freshly ground black pepper

1   Bring the broth to a boil. As the broth is heating, toast the slices of bread to a light brown and set each in the bottom of an ovenproof soup dish.
2   Distribute the broth evenly between the dishes. Now carefully break an egg into each dish, over the slice of bread. Do not split the egg yolk.
3   Put the bowls into a preheated oven at 180°C/350°F/Gas Mark 4 and bake for 10 minutes or until the eggs are just set. Sprinkle each with the fresh Parmesan, season and serve.

Crazy-cut Pasta Romagnola Style

Serves 4
150 g (5 oz) all-purpose flour
3 eggs, beaten
salt
pinch ground nutmeg
1.5 l (3 pt) chicken or beef stock

1   Heap the flour on a work surface, make a well in the middle and add eggs and a pinch of salt and nutmeg. Form into a dough and knead mixture until it is smooth. Form dough into a rectangular loaf shape and leave to dry out a little. Cut it into thick slices and leave to dry a little longer. Chop coarsely and dry out completely. Pour the stock into a saucepan and bring to a boil. Add pasta and cook for 2–3 minutes, then serve in soup bowls.

Tuscan Fish Soup

Serves 4

1 kg (2 lb) assorted fresh whole fish, large
   and small
500 g (1¼ lb) assorted seafood, such as squid,
   shrimp, etc.
400 g (1 lb) mussels or clams
2 tbsp parsley sprigs
3 cloves garlic
1 red chili
olive oil
1 large onion, thinly sliced
1 stick celery thinly sliced
1 carrot, thinly sliced
salt and freshly ground black pepper
120 g (4 oz) dry white wine
3 medium ripe tomatoes, peeled, seeded, sliced
4 large or 8 small slices firm white bread

1 This delicious fish soup can easily be a main course in itself. Any seafood can be used: mullet, eel, shrimp, crayfish etc, provided it is very fresh.

2 Clean fish, keeping heads to one side, leaving small fish whole and cutting big ones into equal-sized chunks. Wash and drain well. Clean and prepare squid; shell and devein shrimp. Then clean mussels or clams, washing very well. Soaking for a couple of hours helps to get rid of any sand.

3 Wash and trim the parsley and chop it together with 2 cloves garlic and the chili. Put this mixture with 4 tbsp oil into a large saucepan over medium heat. Add onion, celery and carrot, season with salt and pepper and fry gently, stirring well. Then add seafood and fish and cook gently, gradually stirring in wine. When wine has evaporated, add mussels or clams. When they have opened, remove and reserve.

4 Add tomatoes and continue cooking until squid is done, adding a little water, if necessary. Meanwhile, poach fish heads separately in water for about 15–20 minutes. Discard bones; push flesh through a strainer or purée in a blender. Stir purée into soup. If mixture is very thick, add a little boiling water. Season to taste.

5 Preheat oven to 190°C/375°F/Gas Mark 5. Rub bread with remaining clove of garlic and put on a baking sheet in oven. When bread has hardened, lay slices in a large tureen or in single soup bowls. When soup is done, remove bones if you wish, correct seasoning and pour over bread. Serve immediately, accompanied by the same wine you have used for cooking.

PASTA, GNOCCHI AND POLENTA

For many people, Italian food means just one thing – pasta. Of course, this amazingly versatile ingredient is the basis for some of the most delicious dishes in Italian cuisine – what could be more typical than the ever popular Lasagne al Forno or Spaghetti with Clams? But just as delicious and just as versatile are gnocchi and polenta – dumplings and cornmeal – which feature in some great Italian classics.

Macaroni with Cheese with Bacon

Serves 4

175 g (6 oz) short-cut macaroni
salt and freshly ground black pepper
½ tsp oil
1 tbsp butter
600 ml (1 pt) Mornay Sauce (see page 87)
50 g (2 oz) cheese (combination of ricotta,
    pecorino and mozzarella)
1 tbsp fresh breadcrumbs
4 slices bacon
2 tomatoes, sliced

1   Preheat the oven to 200°C/400°F/Gas Mark 6.
    Cook the macaroni for 7 minutes in boiling salted
    water to which a few drops of oil have been
    added. Drain well.
2   Preheat the oven to 200°C/400°F/Gas Mark 6.
    Butter an ovenproof dish and prepare the sauce.
    Mix the macaroni with the sauce and pour into the
    dish. Sprinkle with the cheeses mixed with
    fresh breadcrumbs.
3   Arrange the bacon slices on top of the macaroni
    alternating with tomato slices. Cook in the oven for
    15–20 minutes until bacon is cooked.

Hay and Straw with Parma Ham

Serves 4

225 g (8 oz) plain taglierini
225 g (8 oz) green (spinach) taglierini
salt
300 ml (10 fl oz) whipping cream
1 tbsp finely chopped fresh sage
1 tbsp finely fresh parsley, chopped
150 ml (5 fl oz) dry white wine
100 g (4 oz) Parma ham
2 tbsp butter

1   Cook the pastas following the packet instructions.
    Bring the cream to a boil, and then add the sage,
    parsley and dry white wine. Keep boiling to reduce
    the volume of liquid by one-third (to the original
    volume of the cream).
2   When this is done, dice the ham and add it to the
    cream. Remove from the heat.
3   When the pasta is cooked, drain it and whisk in the
    butter. Toss it in the mixture and serve very hot.

Prosciutto
Parma ham, prosciutto, is made from the boned
hind legs of the pig. It is first salted and then dried –
the air in the hills around Parma is ideal to bring it
to maturity. It is sliced paper-thin. The tender, sweet,
light red meat is popularly served as an appetizer
with fresh figs or melon.

Tagliatelle with Pesto

Serves 6
450 g (1 lb) tagliatelle
salt
100 g (4 oz) fresh basil leaves
150 ml (5 fl oz) olive oil
3 tbsp pine nuts
2 cloves garlic
50 g (2 oz) freshly grated Parmesan cheese
3 tbsp freshly grated pecorino cheese (optional)

1 Prepare the pasta in the usual way. To make the pesto put all the ingredients except the cheeses in the blender; process into a fine paste. If you have no blender, use a pestle and mortar. In this case, add the olive oil after you have blended all the other ingredients.

2 Whisk in the cheeses by hand and only then check the salt: the cheeses may well be salty enough. (You may blend the cheeses along with the other ingredients, if you wish, but you will find the texture too smooth if you do).

3 When the pasta is ready, drain it and toss it in the pesto. Sprinkle with more pinenuts and serve.

Tagliatelle Bolognese

Serves 4
1 tbsp oil
1 clove garlic, crushed
1 onion, finely chopped
1 carrot, finely chopped
1 stick celery, finely chopped
200 g (7 oz) canned tomatoes, drained
  and mashed
200 g (7 oz) ground beef
50 g (2 oz) ham
2 tbsp red wine
1 bay leaf
3 chicken livers, chopped
salt and freshly ground black pepper
400 g (14 oz) tagliatelle
Parmesan cheese

1 Put a saucepan on a medium heat and add the
   oil. Add the garlic, onion, carrot and celery and
   cook until browned. Stir in the tomatoes, beef and
   ham and add the red wine to moisten. Tuck the
   bay leaf into the mixture. Cook for a further 20
   minutes.
2 Add the chicken livers and cook for a further 2
   minutes (or until the chicken livers are ready.
   Season, set aside and keep warm.
3 Cook the tagliatelle in the usual way. Drain the
   pasta, pour over the sauce and serve with plenty
   of Parmesan cheese.

Spicy Bacon Pasta

Serves 4
450 g (1 lb) bucatini pasta
1 tbsp olive oil
8 rashers pancetta, chopped
200 g (7 oz) canned tomatoes
1 green chili, chopped
1 tbsp parsley, chopped

1 Boil the pasta in plenty of salted water until al
   dente, drain and put in a serving dish.
2 Heat the oil in a pan and cook the pancetta until
   the fat is browned. Add the tomatoes, chili and
   parsley and cook for 20 minutes, or until the
   tomatoes have reduced to a thick sauce. Pour over
   the pasta and serve.

Spicy Vermicelli

Serves 4–5
450 g (1 lb) vermicelli
8 flat anchovy fillets
1 clove garlic, chopped
vegetable oil
2 red chilies, chopped
1 tbsp parsley, chopped

1   Boil the vermicelli in plenty of salted water until *al dente*, drain and put on a serving dish. Meanwhile, prepare the sauce. Thoroughly rinse the anchovies and pound in a mortar. Fry the garlic in oil until soft. Add the chilies, anchovies and parsley. Pour sauce on the vermicelli and serve

Spaghetti Morgan

Serves 6
450 g (1 lb) dried spaghetti
salt
300 ml (10 fl oz) olive oil
3 cloves garlic
1 medium onion
1 kg (2 lb) fresh plum or canned tomatoes
1 tsp sugar
1 large eggplant
2 tbsp finely chopped fresh basil (2tsp if using dried)

1   Set the water to boil and salt it. As the water is heating, heat 4 tbsp olive oil in a deep frying pan. Crush the garlic, slice the onions and soften them together in the oil.
2   Roughly chop the tomatoes and add them to the onion mixture when it is softened. Add the sugar and turn the heat down to simmer.
3   In a deepish saucepan, heat the remaining olive oil until just below smoking temperature. As the oil heats up, dice the eggplant into 5 mm (¼ in) pieces.
4   Fry the eggplant, a batch at a time, until the flesh is cooked to a wrinkled mid-brown. Set aside the cooked pieces on paper towels. Cook the pasta *al dente*; drain. Stir the eggplant into the tomato sauce and throw in the finely chopped basil. Check the seasoning and serve with the pasta immediately.

Cook's Tip
The pungent flavor of the crisped eggplant, and the fresh and practically uncooked strands of basil make this sauce truly special. It comes originally from Sicily, where it was probably named after the pirate, Henry Morgan.

Spaghetti Carbonara

Serves 4–5

100 g (4 oz) diced pancetta
50 g (2 oz) butter
4 eggs
60 ml (2 fl oz) whipping cream
freshly ground black pepper
450 g (1 lb) spaghetti
50 g (2 oz) grated Parmesan cheese

1   Fry the pancetta in butter, remove with a slotted spoon and keep hot. Beat the eggs in a large bowl with cream and a pinch of pepper.

2   Cook the spaghetti *al dente* in plenty of boiling salted water, drain, pour into a bowl with the eggs and mix well. Sprinkle with the pancetta and Parmesan and serve at once.

Spaghetti with Eggplant

Serves 6
2 medium eggplant
450 g (1 lb) spaghetti
salt
4 tbsp olive oil
3 cloves garlic
1 medium onion
1 kg (2 lb) fresh or canned plum tomatoes
1 tsp sugar
2 tbsp finely chopped basil
  (2 tsp if using dried)
3 tbsp freshly grated Parmesan cheese

1 Preheat the oven to 190°C/350°F/Gas Mark 5. Slice the eggplant lengthways into 1 cm (½ in) strips. Roast them as for Roast Vegetables in Oil (see page 45).
2 Prepare the pasta in the normal manner.
3 Cook half the oil together with the garlic, onion, sugar and tomatoes as for Spaghetti Morgan (see page 66). Add the basil, as soon as the sauce is cooked, after about 20 minutes. When the pasta is cooked, drain it and leave to cool a little.
4 Top each slice of eggplant with a thin layer of pasta. Spread tomato sauce on top of that. Roll the eggplant slice up into a long bundle. Secure it with a toothpick.
5 Arrange the bundles on a baking tray and brush them with the remaining oil. Sprinkle with the Parmesan and return to the oven and bake until the cheese forms a light crust on top.
6 When serving, spoon over what remains of the sauce.

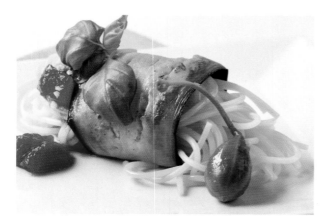

Ravioli with Pumpkin and Sage

450 g (1 lb) pasta dough
2 kg (4¼ lb) pumpkin, seeded
50 g (2 oz) grated Parmesan cheese
4 crushed amaretti cookies
coarse-grained mustard or Italian fruity
  mustard, if available
salt and freshly ground black pepper
pinch of ground nutmeg

For the sauce
100g (4 oz) melted, browned butter
few fresh sage leaves, chopped
30 g (1 oz) grated Parmesan cheese

1 Preheat the oven to 200°C/400°F/Gas Mark 6. Make the pasta, follow the instructions on page 39, mixing a pinch of salt with the flour.
2 For the filling, bake the pumpkin until tender and scrape the flesh into a bowl.
3 Mash the pumpkin well. Stir in the Parmesan, amaretti cookies, and the mustard. Season with salt, pepper and a pinch of nutmeg and mix well.
4 To prepare ravioli, make according to the instructions on page 39, placing the filling at 5–6 cm (2–2½ in) intervals.
5 For the sauce, melt the butter over a medium heat and add in the fresh sage leaves. Stir in the Parmesan.
6 Boil the ravioli in plenty of salted water for approximately 7 minutes or until they rise to the surface of the water and lose their pasty appearance. Drain and add the ravioli to the sauce.
7 Coat the ravioli in the sauce before serving with a sprinkling of more Parmesan cheese.

Veal and Chicken Ravioli

Serves 4

1 small onion, peeled
1 clove garlic
2 tbsp oil
100 g (4 oz) ground veal
50 g (2 oz) cooked chicken
1 tbsp fresh breadcrumbs
1 tbsp Parmesan cheese
salt and freshly ground black pepper
½ tsp brandy (optional)
1 tsp parsley, chopped
few spikes of fresh rosemary
few leaves or 1 tsp dried thyme
½ egg, beaten

1   Dice the onion finely and crush the garlic. Heat the oil and cook the onion and garlic for 4 minutes over low heat until transparent. Remove with a slotted spoon into a bowl.
2   Place the veal in the oil and fry over medium heat for 5 minutes, separating with a fork as it cooks; add the chicken for the last 2 minutes. Spoon into the bowl.
3   Add all the remaining ingredients and mix well with the egg. Leave to cool and use as required for stuffing pasta.

Gratin of Ravioli and Cream

Serves 4

450 g (1 lb) pasta dough
2 tbsp chopped onion
3 tbsp butter
350 g (12 oz) finely diced sausage
2 tbsp breadcrumbs
salt and freshly ground black pepper
2 egg yolks
2 tbsp grated Parmesan cheese

For the sauce

100 g (4 oz) butter
5 tbsp grated Parmesan cheese
about 300 ml (½ pt) half and half

1   Preheat the oven to 200°C/400°F/Gas Mark 6. For the pasta, follow the instructions on page 34, mixing a pinch of salt with the flour.
2   For the filling, soften the onion in butter, add in the sausage, breadcrumbs and salt and pepper and cook gently for 10 minutes. Transfer the sauce to a bowl and allow it to cool. Mix in the egg yolks and Parmesan.
3   Assemble the ravioli according to the instructions in the Ravioli with Pumpkin and Sage recipe on page 68. Boil the ravioli in plenty of salted water for about 7 minutes or until they rise to the surface of the water and lose their pasty appearance.
4   Drain and arrange in a baking dish in layers; dot each layer with butter, sprinkle with Parmesan and drizzle with cream. Bake until golden brown.

Gnocchi with Gorgonzola

Serves 4–6
450 g (1 lb) potato gnocchi (see page 40)
salt
200 ml (7 fl oz) milk
4 tbsp butter
100 g (4 oz) Gorgonzola, crumbled into
   tiny pieces
2 tbsp freshly grated Parmesan cheese
4 tbsp whipping cream

1 Boil the gnocchi as you would pasta, in salted
   water. But watch, as they will cook more quickly –
   3 to 4 minutes should be sufficient.
2 As the gnocchi are cooking, heat the milk in a
   saucepan large enough to hold all the ingredients,
   including the gnocchi. As soon as the milk comes
   to a boil, reduce the heat to a low simmer. Add
   the butter, the crumbled Gorgonzola and the
   Parmesan. Slowly beat everything into a creamy
   paste. Remove from the heat.
3 As soon as the gnocchi is cooked, drain it and add it
   to the sauce. Over a very low heat, stir in the cream.
   Serve instantly.

Fried Polenta with Mushrooms

Serves 6
2 tbsp olive oil
2 tbsp butter
675 g (1½ lb) field or wood mushrooms or ceps
   (porcini mushrooms), roughly chopped
2 cloves garlic, roughly chopped
2 whole small chili peppers, roughly chopped
4 tbsp red wine
1 medium tomato, roughly diced
1 tbsp finely fresh parsley, chopped
1 tbsp finely chopped fresh sage
350 g (¾ lb) cooked and cooled polenta
   (see page 41)
salt and pepper to taste

1   Melt one-third of the oil and the butter together
    over medium heat. Add the mushrooms, garlic
    and chilies and fry together for 3–4 minutes over
    high heat. Add the wine, tomatoes, parsley and
    sage to the mixture. Reduce to a simmer.
2   As the mixture is cooking, slice the cold set polenta
    into manageable blocks and carefully cut each
    block into 2.5 cm (1 in) slices.
3   In a large, open saucepan, heat the remaining oil
    over high heat. Fry each slice on both sides until a
    thin crust forms. Keep the slices hot if you do the
    frying in more than one batch.
4   When all the polenta is fried, season the
    mushroom mixture and spoon it generously over
    each slice. Serve immediately.

Vegetable Lasagne

Serves 4
4 tbsp oil
1 eggplant, sliced
1 red pepper, seeded
1 zucchini, sliced
100 g (4 oz) mushrooms, sliced
salt and freshly ground black pepper
500 ml (17 fl oz) Tomato Sauce (see page 88)
600 ml (1 pt) Béchamel Sauce (page 85)
9 sheets lasagne
50 g (2 oz) cheese (combination of ricotta,
   pecorino and mozzarella)

1   Preheat the oven to 180°C/350°F/Gas Mark 4.
    Heat the oil and fry the vegetables over low heat,
    filling the saucepan and turning in the oil for about
    3 minutes for each batch. You will need to allow 15
    minutes for preparing and frying the vegetables.
2   Start by layering the tomato sauce and one-third
    of the vegetables. Top with Béchamel sauce
    and lasagne. Season and continue layering as
    in Lasagne al Forno (see page 73), ending with
    Béchamel sauce and cheese on top.
3   When all the ingredients are used, bake until
    golden brown in the oven (about 25 minutes).

Lasagne with Spinach and Ricotta

Serves 4

olive oil
1 onion, finely chopped
1 garlic clove, minced
200 g (7 oz) tinned chopped tomatoes
salt and freshly ground black pepper
1 kg (2 lb) fresh spinach
200 ml (1/3 pt) cream
225 g (8 oz) ricotta cheese
fresh nutmeg, for grating
10–12 sheets lasagne
50 g (2 oz) freshly grated Parmesan cheese

1   180°C/350°F/Gas Mark 4. Heat 1 tbsp oil in a frying pan over medium heat and add the chopped onions. Sauté for 5–10 minutes or until softened. Add the garlic and cook for a further 30 seconds. Stir in the chopped tomatoes, season to taste, and bring to a boil. Simmer for 10 more minutes; set aside.

2   Wash the spinach and discard any tough stalks or discoloured leaves. Transfer the wet spinach to a large saucepan and place over low heat. Cook gently, stirring occasionally, until the leaves are completely wilted. Drain in a sieve, pressing down on the cooked spinach with a wooden spoon to ensure that all the cooking water has been removed.

3   Chop the cooked spinach and transfer to a mixing bowl. Add the cream and ricotta, and grate in a little fresh nutmeg. Season to taste. Mix together well.

4   Place a layer of lasagne sheets in the bottom of a lightly oiled oblong ovenproof dish. Add a layer of spinach and ricotta mixture. Continue layering lasagne and spinach mixture in the same way until you have no spinach mixture left. Add grated Parmesan cheese to the top layer.

5   Pour over the reserved tomato sauce. Transfer the dish to the oven and cook for 20–30 minutes or until the pasta is cooked (insert a skewer in the dish to test for this; the skewer should pass through the pasta with ease). Remove from the oven once done and leave to cool slightly before serving.

Chicken and Mushroom Lasagne

Serves 4–6
1 onion, peeled and diced
2 tbsp butter
100 g (4 oz) mushrooms, washed and sliced
350 g (12 oz) cooked chicken, diced
600 ml (1 pt) Béchamel Sauce (see page 85)
25 g (1 oz) grated Parmesan cheese
9 sheets lasagne
salt and freshly ground white pepper
2 tbsp fresh breadcrumbs

1 Preheat the oven to 180°C/350°F/Gas Mark 4. Cook the onion in the butter over low heat for about 3 minutes. Add the mushrooms and cook for 2 more minutes. Add the chicken to the mushroom and onions, season well. Make up the Béchamel sauce, season well.

2 Place about 4 tbsp sauce in the bottom of an ovenproof dish. Cover with one third of the chicken mixture. Place sheets of lasagne on top to cover.

3 Place 4 tbsp sauce on top of the lasagne and one-third of the chicken mixture. Continue with the third layer of lasagne, and top with the remaining Béchamel sauce.

4 Mix the fresh breadcrumbs with the remaining cheese and sprinkle on top. Bake in the oven for 25 minutes until golden brown.

Lasagne al Forno

Serves 6
450 g (1 lb) dried lasagne
salt
4 tbsp olive oil
2 cloves garlic
1 medium onion
1 kg (2 lb) fresh or canned plum tomatoes
fresh parsley, chopped
1 tsp sugar
2 tbsp fresh basil (or 2tsp dried)
600 ml (1 pt) Béchamel Sauce (see page 85)

1 Preheat the oven to 220°C/425°F/Gas Mark 7. Cook the strips of lasagne until just soft in a large saucepan of salted boiling water and a little olive oil. Remove from the water, drain them, and lay them out, not overlapping, on a lightly greased work surface.

2 Using a little over half of the oil, make Tomato Sauce (see page 88).

3 Grease the bottom of a 30 cm (12 in) baking dish with the remaining oil. Cover it with a layer of the cooked pasta.

4 Spoon a layer of the tomato sauce onto the pasta, followed by a layer of the Béchamel. Proceed until the dish is full: pasta, sauce, Béchamel, pasta, sauce and so on. (Ensure you retain enough Béchamel for a generous final coating).

5 Bake in the oven for 15–20 minutes, or until the top has browned and begun to crisp at the edges.

Ricotta and Parmesan Cannelloni

Serves 4

450g (1 lb) pasta dough (see page 34), rolled out
   and cut into 100 mm x 140 mm lengths
225 g (8 oz) ricotta cheese
50 g (2 oz) Parmesan cheese
2 tbsp parsley, chopped
1 tbsp fresh breadcrumbs
¼ tsp nutmeg
½ tsp marjoram
salt and freshly ground black pepper
1 egg, beaten

1 Preheat the oven to 180°C/350°F/Gas Mark 4. Mix all the ingredients in a bowl, except the pasta, adding the egg slowly so that the mixture does not become too wet. Make sure you leave enough cheese to cover the cannelloni once in the dish.

2 Take a pasta length and spoon some of the mixture one third of the way across the width. Roll the length of the pasta around the mixture to make the cannelloni.

3 Place the rolled cannelloni into an ovenproof dish and pour over any remaining cheese mixture, plus freshly grated cheese.

Variation

Ricotta and Spinach Stuffing (see image above): Use 700 g (7 oz) ricotta cheese. Drain 100g (4 oz) fresh, frozen or tinned spinach. Chop spinach and mix with all other ingredients.

Pasta Trio

Serves 4
225 g (8 oz) stuffed ravioli or tortellini
300 ml (10 fl oz) Béchamel Sauce (see page 85)
225 g (8 oz) tagliatelli
225 ml (8 fl oz) Quick Tomato Sauce (see page 89)
225 g (8 oz) wholemeal fusili
300 ml (10 fl oz) Bolognese Sauce (see page 91)
100 g (4 oz) Parmesan cheese, to garnish

1 For this dish you can serve any of your favorite pastas and sauces.
2 Cook the pasta, starting with the one with the longest cooking time, drain the water into a bowl and return the pasta to the saucepan and keep it warm.
3 Keep the three sauces warm. Serve on single dishes on a large plate accompanied by a bowl of Parmesan cheese and green salad.

Macaroni with Shrimp

Serves 4
1 tsp dried thyme
1 bay leaf
2 tbsp parsley, chopped
salt
200 g uncooked shrimp (unshelled)
450 g (1 lb) macaroni
2 cloves garlic, crushed
vegetable oil
1 red chili, chopped
400 g (14 oz) peeled, chopped tomatoes

1 Put the thyme, bay leaf, 1 tbsp parsley and a pinch of salt into a saucepan of water, bring to a boil and add the shrimp. Cook for 3 minutes, then drain. Shell, devein and coarsely chop the shrimp. Cook the macaroni *al dente* in plenty of boiling salted water.
2 Fry the garlic in oil, add chili pepper and tomatoes, season with salt and cook for 10 minutes. Add the shrimp.
3 Drain the pasta, mix in the sauce and sprinkle on the remaining parsley.

Linguini and Mussels

Serves 4

1 tbsp olive oil

1 garlic clove, minced

200 g (7 oz) tinned tomatoes, drained and
   mashed

½ tsp dried basil, or fresh snipped basil to taste

freshly ground black pepper

225 g (8 oz) peeled raw shrimp

salt

500 ml (1 pt) mussels, scrubbed clean

1 glass dry white wine

2 tbsp chopped parsley

400 g (14 oz) linguini

a few cooked, unpeeled shrimp

1 Heat the oil in a large frying pan over medium heat and add the garlic. Sauté for a few seconds then add the tomatoes, basil, pepper and peeled shrimp. Cook for a few more minutes until the shrimp have turned pink.

2 Bring a large pan of salted water to a boil. While you are waiting, sort through the mussels and discard any that are open or broken. Scrub the remaining mussels clean and then place in a large saucepan and pour on the white wine. Add 1 tbsp chopped parsley, cover and place over medium heat. Bring to a simmer and cook for 5–10 minutes, until the mussels open. Discard any mussels that do not open.

3 Once the pan of water for the pasta has come to a boil, add the pasta. Bring back to a boil and cook for 8–10 minutes or until *al dente*.

4 Set aside some of the mussels in their shells as garnish. Remove the remaining cooked mussels from their shells and stir in with the shrimp and tomato sauce. You can add a little of the mussel-cooking liquid to the sauce to thin it if desired. If you do this, strain the liquid through a fine sieve first.

5 Just before the pasta is ready, reheat the sauce. When the pasta is cooked, drain and return to the saucepan. Add the shrimp, mussel and tomato sauce and mix well. Transfer to serving plates and serve garnished with the remaining parsley, the unpeeled shrimp and the reserved mussels.

Seafood Spaghetti Baked in Foil

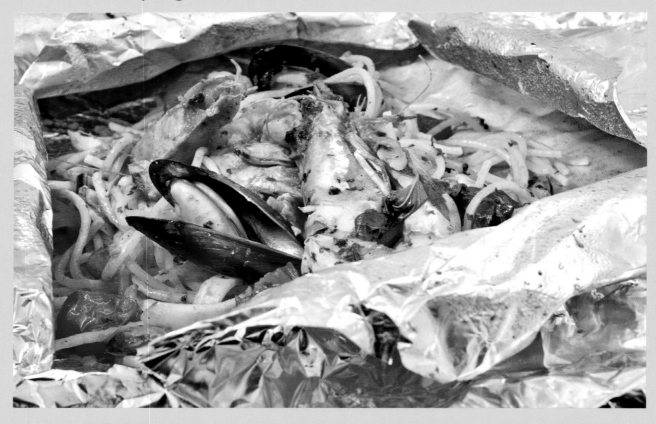

Serves 6
450 g (1 lb) spaghetti
200 g cherry tomatoes
2 tbsp fresh parsley, finely chopped
diced red chili
225 g (8 oz) peeled uncooked large shrimp
handful of mussels
freshly grated black pepper

1   Preheat the oven to 190°C/375°F/Gas Mark 5. Set the pasta to cook in the usual way.
2   As the pasta is cooking, heat the tomatoes in a saucepan. Add the parsley and chili, and season.
3   Add the shrimp and mussels to the tomato sauce and gently heat.
4   When you are ready to drain the pasta, spread out on a baking tray a sheet of foil large enough to fold over and completely envelop both pasta and sauce. Place the drained pasta in the middle of the foil and pour the sauce on top. Lift the edges of the foil upwards around the pasta and fold them together, completely sealing the contents.
5   Bake the parcel in the hot oven for about 5 minutes, then transfer the foil intact to a serving dish. Unseal at the table, sprinkle with black pepper and serve.

Spaghetti with Clams

Serves 4
1 onion, peeled
2 cloves garlic, crushed
4 tbsp olive oil
6 beef tomatoes, peeled and diced, or
    400 g (15 oz) canned tomatoes
4 tbsp white wine
salt and freshly ground black pepper
1 small can clams
350 g (12 oz) spaghetti
1 tbsp butter
pinch of nutmeg
2 tbsp fresh parsley, chopped

1   Dice the onion finely, peel and crush the garlic. Heat the oil in a saucepan or large frying pan and cook over low heat until the onion is transparent.
2   Add the tomatoes, white wine and seasoning. Simmer for 10 minutes. Add the drained clams and heat gently for 6 more minutes.
3   Meanwhile, cook the spaghetti in plenty of boiling salted water for about 12 minutes. Drain and toss in a little melted butter, add a shake of pepper and nutmeg.
4   Add the parsley to the sauce and stir well. Combine with the clam sauce and serve at once on heated plates.

Cook's Tip
To cook fresh clams, scrub the shells and wash well in several batches of cold water to remove sand and grit. Place them in a frying pan with 2 tbsp white wine and cook over a high heat until the shells open. Strain and use the juice in the sauce. Remove the fish from the shells and heat the sauce through as above.

Spaghetti with Chicken Livers

Serves 4
450 g (1 lb) chicken livers, diced
1 red pepper, seeded
1 clove garlic, crushed
4 tbsp butter
4 tomatoes, skinned and chopped
2 basil leaves, chopped
salt and freshly ground black pepper
450 g (1 lb) spaghetti
oil
fresh parsley, chopped (optional)

1   Prepare the chicken livers by cutting into small pieces. Dice the pepper finely. Blanch it for 2 minutes in water that has just boiled and drain. Crush the garlic.
2   Melt the butter in a frying pan and simmer the garlic and pepper for 5 minutes. Add the chicken livers and stir, mixing with the pepper. Cook for 5–6 minutes on a low heat. Add the tomatoes, basil and seasoning.
3   While the sauce is simmering, cook the spaghetti in boiling salted water with a few drops of oil. Drain and mix well with the chicken liver sauce. Each portion can be garnished with some freshly chopped parsley.

Gnocchi with Chicken Livers

Serves 4–6

450 g (1 lb) potato gnocchi
salt
2 tbsp olive oil
2 cloves garlic
1 small onion, very finely chopped
1 tbsp finely chopped fresh sage
150 ml (5 fl oz) red wine
225 g (8 oz) chicken livers
150 ml (5 fl oz) heavy cream

1 Cook the gnocchi in the usual way, in salted boiling water.

2 Heat the oil in a frying pan, throw in the whole cloves of garlic and the onion. Soften in the oil until the onion begins to brown.

3 Add the sage and the red wine; reduce the volume of the wine by half over high heat. Remove.

4 When all the gnocchi are ready, bring the red wine mixture back to a boil and add the livers, very finely chopped. Cook for a minute or so, then add the cream.

5 Bring the sauce back to a boil, check the seasoning and, off the heat, gently stir in the gnocchi. Serve immediately.

SAUCES

Most people enjoy pasta with sauce, and combining the more unusual sauces – as well as the old favorites – with different pastas, adds endless variety to everyday meals. The Italians are known for their use of fresh young vegetables and it is these ingredients that make even the most simple sauce, served with pasta, a feast. When preparing sauces with vegetables, remember to serve pasta of a similar size to that of the sauce ingredients as it is difficult to pick up small pasta with chunky vegetables.

Olive Oil

Olive oil is used in those parts of Italy where the climate suits the cultivation of olive trees; in the cooler, wetter northern regions, butter is favored. Each olive growing region produces its own variety of oil with its own distinct characteristics. Tuscan olive oil is probably the most renowned; connoisseurs often claim that the oil produced around Lucca, in Tuscany, is the best in the country. Tuscan oil has a strong, slightly peppery flavor and so works well when combined with tomatoes and bean dishes. Oil from Liguria is light in flavor and so won't overpower other foods, making it ideal for sauces – such as pesto – where you want the flavor of the other ingredients to shine. Puglian olive oil is a good general purpose oil with a strong flavor. It's suitable for frying and roasting meats and is an excellent oil for coating vegetables such as peppers and eggplant prior to roasting. However, the Italian olive oil on sale in most stores is a blend of several varieties. Just as with

wine, olive oil from a specific producer – often known as single-estate oil – will cost considerably more. That said, it is worth buying the most expensive oil you can afford, especially for salads and other dishes where the oil is uncooked and where you will appreciate its distinctive flavor. For everyday Italian cooking you can use a blended oil, but you should choose the best quality available. Look for extra-virgin or virgin olive oil. Both of these are obtained from the first pressing of the olives and are unrefined. Extra-virgin is the best quality, with less that 1 percent acidity; virgin olive oil has 1–2 percent acidity. Oils labeled as pure olive oil, or just as olive oil, contain oil that has been chemically refined, although this may be combined with an amount of virgin olive oil. It goes without saying that the extra-virgin and virgin oils will have the best flavor and should be favored by anyone wanting to cook authentic Italian dishes.

Genoese Pesto

Makes 300 ml (½ pt)
25 g (1 oz) fresh basil leaves
2 cloves garlic
100 ml (4 fl oz) olive oil
50 g (2 oz) pine nuts
50 g (2 oz) Parmesan cheese
pinch of salt

1 Blend the basil leaves in a blender. Add the crushed cloves of garlic and olive oil. Process for a few seconds. Gradually add the pine nuts and Parmesan cheese. Season, remembering that Parmesan has a salty taste. The consistency should be thick and creamy.

2 This quantity of pesto will be enough for 450 g (1 lb) cooked drained pasta. To cook with pasta melt 2 tbsp butter in the saucepan and re-heat the cooked pasta. Remove from the heat and mix 2 tbsp pesto with the pasta. Serve on single plates with a spoonful of pesto on each helping. Parmesan can be added last.

3 The pesto is never heated. It can be served on pasta at the table but make sure the pasta is hot when served.

Salsa Verde

This sharp green sauce is often served with boiled meats or white fish. Use vinegar for a meat sauce and lemon juice for a fish one. Blend together 4 tbsp olive oil and 1 tbsp each of parsley and capers, 2 anchovy fillets, ½ clove garlic and 1 tsp of red wine vinegar or lemon juice.

Winter Pesto Sauce

Makes 300 ml (½ pt)
50 g (2 oz) fresh parsley
2 cloves garlic
50 g (2 oz) pine nuts
50 g (2 oz) Parmesan cheese
salt and freshly ground black pepper
2 tsp dried basil
150 ml (5 fl oz) olive oil

1 Chop the parsley finely with a sharp knife. In a blender put the parsley, with the garlic and process for a few seconds. With the blender still running, add the pinenuts, Parmesan, salt and pepper through the top of the machine.

2 When the mixture is puréed add olive oil, a little at a time. Add the dried basil when half of the oil has been added. Continue adding oil until a thick creamy mixture is made.

Hot Anchovy Dip

Serves 4
100 g (4 oz) anchovy fillets
5 cloves garlic
2 tbsp butter
175 ml (6 fl oz) virgin olive oil
salt

1 Rinse the anchovies well, then pat dry. Cut the garlic into fine slivers or, if preferred, crush it. Put the saucepan over a low flame and add the butter and garlic.
2 Let it cook gently for a few minutes without browning, then gradually add the oil and the anchovies. Blend the anchovies in and cook over very low heat for about 15 minutes, stirring occasionally.
3 Finally taste and add salt, if necessary. Serve in the cooking dish.

Cook's Tip
This hot dip is a speciality of Piedmont. It is brought to the table in a terracotta saucepan and put over a little candle – if possible each person should have his or her own dish. Each person dips crudités or cooked vegetables into the sauce. Use tender white cardoons – a relative of the thistle and the artichoke – soaked first in acidulated cold water; peppers, celery, tender cauliflower, or cooked onions, potatoes, beetroots, carrots and turnips, etc. Make sure the dish is stable to avoid accidents. If you want the garlic to be more digestible, soak it for 2 hours before use in a glass of milk. In some parts of Piedmont it is customary to add crushed pieces of walnut to the dip. Leftovers of the sauce can be served with scrambled eggs.

Pepper Sauce

Makes 600 ml (1 pt)
1 red pepper, seeded
1 green pepper, seeded
1 tbsp parsley, chopped
4tbsp stock or water
300 ml (10 fl oz) tomato sauce, puréed

1 Dice the seeded peppers quite finely. Add to the tomato sauce with 4 tbsp stock or water and simmer for 10 minutes.
2 Add chopped parsley and use either on it own with pasta or alternatively with meat or fish to accompany pasta.

Mayonnaise

Makes 300 ml (½ pt)
2 egg yolks
300 ml (10 fl oz) olive oil
½ tsp salt
pinch white pepper
pinch dried mustard
1 tbsp wine vinegar or lemon juice

1 Make sure the eggs are used at room temperature and not taken directly from the fridge. Warm a clean, dry bowl slightly for the egg yolks, mix for a few seconds. Gradually add the oil, drop by drop to begin with. Mix briskly with a wooden spoon or a small wire whisk. The mixture will become a thick creamy emulsion as the drops of oil are added. When the mixture has thickened add the seasoning with vinegar or lemon juice. Beat well. The mayonnaise can be made thicker or thinner according to the amount of vinegar or lemon juice used. Taste for seasoning before using.

Cook's Tip

The process in making mayonnaise is a chemical one known as "emulsification," in which single molecules of one liquid are held in suspension by another, in this case the oil and egg yolks, respectively.

Work with ingredients at room temperature, never straight from the fridge.

Do not exceed the 2 yolks to 300 ml (10 fl oz) oil ratio. This is all the oil the eggs can "hold."

Go slowly with the oil until you're used to the process. The eggs need a little coaxing to start with.

Béchamel Sauce

Makes 600 ml (1 pt)
600 ml (1 pt) milk
1 small onion, peeled
1 small carrot, peeled and sliced
1 bay leaf
6 slightly crushed peppercorns
1 blade mace
1 stalk parsley
3 tbsp butter
40 g (1½ oz) flour
salt and white pepper

1 Pour the milk into a saucepan. Add the onion, cut into quarters, with two slices of carrot, the bay leaf, peppercorns, mace and parsley stalk.

2 Cover and allow to heat on low heat without boiling for about 10 minutes. Remove from the heat and allow to infuse for 10 more minutes, covered.

3 Make a roux (a blend of butter and flour) by melting the butter in a saucepan. Do not allow the butter to brown. Add the flour and stir well over medium heat.

4 Gradually add the strained milk and stir briskly or whisk until a smooth creamy sauce is made. Season to taste.

Blue Cheese Sauce

Makes 750 ml (1¼ pt)

600 ml (1 pt) Béchamel Sauce (see page 85)
100 g (4 oz) Roquefort or other blue cheese
salt and freshly ground black pepper
½ tsp Dijon mustard
pinch of cayenne pepper
handful chopped walnuts

1 Make the Béchamel sauce. Crumble the blue cheese and add it to the sauce. Stir over low heat.

2 Taste for seasoning. Add salt and pepper to taste and then the mustard. Then stir in the pinch of cayenne and the walnuts.

3 This sauce is enough to accompany approximately 450–750 g (1–1½ lb) cooked pasta.

Spinach and Ricotta Sauce

Makes approximately 600 ml (1 pt)
300 ml (10 fl oz) Béchamel Sauce (see page 85)
225 g (8 oz) (after cooking) fresh or
    frozen spinach
100 g (4 oz) ricotta cheese
½ tsp nutmeg
salt and freshly ground black pepper

1 Make the Béchamel sauce.
2 Cook the spinach for a few minutes and then drain well. Squeeze against the colander to remove the liquid.
3 You will need to cook approx 750 g (1½ lb) fresh spinach to be left with the amount required by the recipe. Chop or purée.
4 Mix the ricotta with the spinach and season well, then add the nutmeg. Gradually stir into the Béchamel sauce and reheat carefully over low heat.
5 Serve with approximately 500–750 g (1–1½ lb) cooked pasta. This sauce is also delicious used in a vegetable or chicken lasagne.

Ricotta

Ricotta is a moist cottage cheese made from sheep's milk and can be either mild or strong, according to the region. In Piedmont and around Rome it is eaten very fresh with pepper and salt, or sometimes with coffee and sugar, sprinkled on it. It can be used in cooking sweet and savory dishes. In southern Italy *ricotta forte* is made from salted sheep's milk. It can be dried in the sun or in an oven and grated for cooking.

Mornay Sauce

Makes 750 ml (1¼ pt)
2 egg yolks
2 tbsp cream
600 ml (1 pt) Béchamel Sauce (see page 85)
50 g (2 oz) grated Parmesan cheese

1 Mix the egg yolks with the cream and add a little warm Béchamel. Return to the warm Béchamel sauce and stir well.
2 Finally in the grated cheese.

Tomato Sauce

Serves 4
2 tbsp oil
1 large onion, peeled and diced
1–2 cloves garlic, peeled and crushed
2 sticks celery, washed
1 carrot, scraped and grated
400 g (15 oz) canned tomatoes
450 g (1 lb) tomatoes, skinned and chopped
1 bouquet garni
1 bay leaf
1 tbsp fresh or ½ tsp dried basil, chopped
1 stalk parsley
½ tsp sugar
300 ml (10 fl oz) chicken or beef stock
2 tbsp red wine
salt and freshly ground black pepper

1. Heat the oil in a saucepan and cook the onions over low heat for 5 minutes until transparent. Add the garlic to the onions.
2. Remove the strings from the celery with a sharp knife and chop into small pieces. Add to the onion.
3. Add all the other ingredients, bring to a boil, lower the heat and simmer for 40 minutes. Remove the bouquet garni, bay leaf and parsley stalk and serve with pasta.
4. For a smooth textured sauce, pass through a sieve or blender.

Tomato and Meat Sauce

Serves 4
3.6 kg (8 lb) firm, ripe tomatoes
450g (1 lb) slender carrots
175 g (6 oz) sliced celery
20 g (1 oz) mixed parsley, sage and basil, chopped
5 cloves garlic, crushed
450 g (1 lb) onions, thinly sliced
50 g (2 oz) butter
5 tbsp olive oil
750 g (1½ lb) lean minced beef
tomato juice
salt

1   Cook the tomato sauce by putting the tomatoes, carrots, celery, herbs and garlic in a large saucepan. Heat gently and when they have reached simmering point, cover and cook for 2½ hours, stirring occasionally.
2   Put the onions in a saucepan with butter and olive oil. Heat gently until softened, add the meat and cook for 1½ hours, adding a little tomato juice if necessary. Combine the meat sauce with the tomato sauce and cook for 1 hour longer, then season with salt.

Quick Tomato Sauce

Serves 4
4 tbsp olive oil
2 cloves garlic, crushed
1½ kg (3 lb) ripe beef tomatoes, peeled and chopped
salt and freshly ground black pepper
6 basil leaves

1   Heat the oil in a saucepan, add the garlic and stir for 1 minute. Add the tomatoes and seasoning and allow the sauce to simmer for 6 minutes.
2   Chop the basil leaves and add to the tomatoes, stirring the sauce for one more minute. Serve on freshly cooked pasta.

Tomatoes
Though an indispensable ingredient in Italian cooking, the tomato was introduced into the country only comparatively recently. The Italians grow either plum tomatoes or the huge, curved, irregular Marmande variety – both have infinitely more flavor than the pale, insipid specimens cultivated in Britain and America. Many Italians bottle their own tomatoes and make their own tomato concentrate at home for use during the winter months. Those who have neither the time nor the space use the canned variety.

Puttanesca Sauce

Serves 4

1 onion, peeled and diced

2 tbsp oil

1 clove garlic, crushed

1 carrot, scraped and chopped

400 g (15 oz) canned tomatoes

2 tomatoes, skinned and chopped

4 tbsp white wine

1 bay leaf

3–4 basil leaves or 1 tsp dried basil

salt and freshly ground pepper

1 small can anchovies

1 tbsp capers, chopped

50 g (2 oz) pitted black olives

3 drops Tabasco sauce

1 tbsp freshly parsley, chopped

1 Put the onion into the oil in a frying pan over low heat. Allow to cook gently for 4 minutes, then add the crushed garlic and carrots. Stir in the oil for another minute, add the tomatoes, white wine, bay leaf, basil, some seasoning and 4 anchovy fillets. Bring to a boil and simmer for 30 minutes. Sieve or purée into a measuring cup. Return to the saucepan and add chopped capers, the remainder of the anchovies chopped into small pieces, chopped olives and the Tabasco sauce. Reheat gently.

2 Serve with 450 g (1 lb) cooked pasta, with Parmesan cheese on the side.

Bolognese Sauce

Serves 4

1 large onion, peeled and diced
1 carrot, peeled and diced
1 stick celery, washed and diced
2 cloves garlic, crushed
2 slices bacon
1 tbsp oil
100 g (4 oz) lean ground beef
100 g (4 oz) lean ground veal
300 ml (10 fl oz) beef stock or water
400 g (15 oz) canned tomatoes
4 tomatoes, skinned and chopped
1 bay leaf
1 tsp oregano
½ tsp basil
1 bouquet garni
salt and freshly ground black pepper
1 tbsp tomato paste
150 ml (5 fl oz) red wine

1   Prepare the vegetables, making sure that they are diced very finely. Remove the strings from the celery with a sharp knife before chopping. Crush the garlic. Cut the bacon into small pieces, after removing the rind.

2   Heat the oil in the saucepan and brown all the meat over medium heat. Remove with a slotted spoon, leaving any fat behind. Cook the vegetables in the meat fat, adding a little extra oil if necessary, over low heat for 5 minutes.

3   Put the meat and vegetables into a saucepan with the stock, tomatoes, herbs and seasoning. Lastly add the tomato paste and stir in the wine.

4   Bring to a boil and simmer gently for 45 minutes. Remove the bouquet garni and bay leaf before serving.

5   Serve with spaghetti and other pastas, with Parmesan cheese served separately.

Ragu Sauce

Serves 4

1 onion, peeled
2 cloves garlic, crushed
1 carrot, scraped and grated
1 stick celery
6 tomatoes, peeled and chopped or 400 g
   (15 oz) canned tomatoes
4 tbsp olive oil
225 g (8 oz) lean ground beef
100 g (4 oz) chicken livers
1 bouquet garni
1 bay leaf
1 tsp oregano
1 stalk parsley
300 ml (10 fl oz) stock and red wine
salt and freshly ground black pepper

1. Prepare the vegetables. Chop the onion finely, crush the garlic and coarsely grate the carrot. Wash the celery and remove strings with a sharp knife before chopping into very small pieces. Prepare the tomatoes.

2. Heat half of the oil in a saucepan and cook the onion and garlic for 3 minutes over low heat. Add the carrot and celery, stir into the oil and let cook for 3 more minutes.

3. Heat the remaining oil in a frying pan and brown the beef well over high heat. Turn the heat down to medium and add the chopped chicken livers. Mix with the beef and cook until brown.

4. Add the meat to the vegetables with the herbs, stock and wine, season well, and simmer for 45 minutes. Taste for seasoning before serving with freshly cooked pasta.

Tuna and Mushroom Sauce

Makes 750 ml (1¼ pt)

2 tbsp butter

1 tbsp olive oil

100 g (4 oz) mushrooms, washed

200 g (7 oz) canned tuna

2 tsp tomato paste

2 tbsp white wine

600 ml (1 pt) Béchamel Sauce (see page 85)

salt and freshly ground black pepper

1 Heat the butter and oil and cook the mushrooms for 3 minutes, turning from time to time.

2 Flake the tuna. Add the tomato paste and white wine to the Béchamel sauce. Mix well.

3 Over low heat, reheat the sauce and gradually stir in the tuna and the drained mushrooms. Cook gently for a few minutes until well mixed and hot. Taste and adjust seasoning.

4 Mix the sauce with 450 g (1 lb) cooked pasta such as tagliatelle.

RICE

In the north of Italy, rice, rather than pasta, is the main staple. Here, it is used to make risotto – where the typical short-grain rice of these regions is combined with other ingredients to create rich, tasty dishes. To make a risotto, you stir the rice as it cooks – this releases starch, which helps give the dish its characteristic moist and creamy texture. Serve risottos in wide soup bowls or pasta plates.

Chicken Risotto

Serves 4

1½ kg (3 lb) chicken, cooked, giblets reserved
50 g (5 oz) chopped veal
1 carrot, chopped
1 onion, chopped
1 stick celery, chopped
salt
6 tbsp butter
freshly ground black pepper
250 ml (8 fl oz) dry white wine
3 medium tomatoes, chopped
290 g (10½ oz) rice
4 tbsp grated Parmesan cheese

1   Skin and de-bone the chicken; dice the flesh and set aside. Put the veal, chicken bones and giblets into a saucepan with half of the carrot, onion and celery. Cover with water, add a pinch of salt and cook over medium heat for about 30 minutes. Strain this stock, set aside and keep hot.

2   In a second saucepan, lightly brown the remaining chopped vegetables in half of the butter. Add the diced chicken, season with salt and pepper and continue cooking, covered, for a few minutes. Pour in the wine, reduce by half, add the tomatoes and cook until soft.

3   Pour in the rice and add a ladleful of the stock. Continue adding stock at intervals as the rice dries out. When it is cooked, remove from the heat, stir in the remaining butter and half the Parmesan. Let stand for a minute and then serve with the remaining Parmesan cheese.

Risotto with Two Cheeses

Serves 4

4 tbsp butter
1 medium onion, finely sliced
300 g (11 oz) Arborio (risotto) rice
2 chicken stock cubes or 900 ml (2 pt) Pastine in Brodo (see page 52)
50 g (2 oz) freshly grated Parmesan cheese
150 ml (5 fl oz) whipping cream
50 g (2 oz) crumbled Gorgonzola
salt and freshly ground black pepper

1   Melt the butter in a heavy saucepan and soften the onion in it. Add the rice and toast it for 2–3 minutes.

2   Crumble in the stock and add 900 ml (2 pt) water. Cook the rice until it is *al dente*. Add the Parmesan.

3   As the rice is cooking, warm the cream and add the crumbled Gorgonzola to it. Stir until the cheese has thoroughly melted.

4   When the rice is cooked, whisk in the cream and Gorgonzola, season and serve piping hot.

Risotto with Dried Porcini Mushrooms

Serves 4–6
50 g (2 oz) dried porcini mushrooms
300 ml (10 fl oz) dry white wine
Pastine in Brodo (see page 52) or 1 chicken stock
   cube or 1 l (2 pt)
1 small onion
4 tbsp olive oil
400 g (14 oz) Arborio (risotto) rice
150 ml (5 fl oz) whipping cream
3 tbsp freshly grated Parmesan cheese
salt and freshly ground black pepper

1 Put the dried mushrooms in a saucepan and cover them with the wine. Add the pastine in brodo, or crumble the stock cube over them and add 1 l (2 pt) water.

2 Poach the mushrooms gently in the stock and wine until they are soft and swollen. Strain them carefully and reserve the poaching liquid. Wash the mushrooms once or twice more in fresh water: they can be gritty.

3 To remove grit from the poaching liquid, strain it too, either through muslin or a very fine strainer.

4 Boil the poaching liquid briskly. Your aim is to reduce its volume by about one-third to intensify its flavor.

5 As the mushroom stock boils, finely slice the onion, then soften it in a heavy saucepan with the oil. Add the rice and toast it with the oil and onion.

6 Pour the mushroom liquid over the rice and let it cook until the liquid is almost absorbed. If this happens before the rice is cooked – about 15 minutes – add small amounts of water.

7 When the rice is cooked, stir in the cream and cheese; check the seasoning. Just before serving, stir in the mushrooms.

Milanese Risotto

Serves 4
2 tbsp beef marrow
1 small onion, thinly sliced
150 g (5 oz) butter
350 g (12 oz) rice
250 ml (8 fl oz) dry white wine
1.2 l (2½ pt) beef stock, skimmed of fat
⅛ tsp saffron
5 tbsp grated Parmesan cheese

1   Scrape the marrow with a knife to remove any bits of bone, then chop and put in a saucepan with the onion and 65 g (2½ oz) butter. Fry until the onion is soft but not brown. Add the rice and fry for 2 or 3 minutes. Add the wine and cook until absorbed. Add the stock with a ladle, waiting between each addition until it has been absorbed. Cook the rice for 30 minutes.

2   Ten minutes before the end of cooking time, dissolve the saffron in a few tbsp boiling stock and add to the rice. Finally, add the remaining butter and stir in the Parmesan. Let it stand, covered, for 2 minutes before serving.

Saffron
Saffron gives its lovely color to Milan's famous risotto. It comes from the pistils of the autumn flowering crocus. Half a million pistils are needed to make about 1 kg (2 lb) of saffron powder, so it is very expensive.

Country-style Risotto

Serves 4
vegetable oil
1 onion, chopped
65 g (2½ oz) shelled fresh peas
50 g (2 oz) asparagus tips
90 g (3½ oz) sliced zucchini
chicken or beef stock
450 g (1 lb) chopped tomatoes
65 g (2½ oz) cooked navy beans
salt and freshly ground black pepper
350 g (12 oz) rice
5 tbsp butter
6 tbsp grated Parmesan cheese

1   Heat a little oil in a saucepan, add the onion and cook until soft. Add the peas, asparagus and zucchini and cook for about 5 minutes. Add a little stock and cook over low heat for 10 minutes.

2   Add the tomatoes and beans; season with salt and pepper. Cook for 15 minutes, then add the rice. Stir and add further stock, as necessary, and cook until *al dente*.

3   Stir in the butter and 3 tbsp Parmesan. Serve sprinkled with the remaining Parmesan.

Artichoke Risotto

Serves 4
4 tbsp butter
1 small onion, finely sliced
350 g (12 oz) Arborio (risotto) rice
Pastine in Brodo (see page 52) or 2 chicken stock
    cubes or 1.25 l (2½ pt)
2 cans artichoke hearts
4 tbsp whipping cream
3 tbsp freshly grated Parmesan cheese
salt and freshly ground black pepper

1   Melt the butter in a heavy saucepan. Soften
    the onion in it. Add the rice and toast it for
    2–3 minutes. (Do not allow either rice or onion
    to colour).
2   Add pastine in brodo, or crumble in the stock
    cube and add 1¼ l (2½ pt) water. Cook the rice
    until it is *al dente*. If too much liquid remains in
    the saucepan, ladle it out.
3   As the rice is cooking, drain and wash the
    artichoke hearts. Gently warm them with the
    cream and the grated Parmesan. Fold this
    mixture into the rice as soon as it is cooked.
    Season and serve immediately.

Cook's Tip
The dish Artichoke Risotto originates with baby
artichokes – which can be eaten whole, choke and
all – in season in Italy during very early spring. If you
can find them, use them. Regrettably, they are very
rare outside Italy.

Sicilian Artichoke Risotto

Serves 4
5 tbsp coarsely chopped bacon
1 onion
1 clove garlic
½ stick celery
.1 bunch parsley
vegetable oil
100 g (4 oz) peeled, seeded, chopped tomato
salt and freshly ground black pepper
275 g (10 oz) tinned artichoke hearts, drained
600 ml (1 pt) cold water
225 g (8 oz) Arborio rice
25 g (1 oz) grated Pecorino cheese

1   Chop together the bacon, onion, garlic, celery
    and parsley and fry in a few tbsp oil. Then add the
    tomato, season with salt and pepper and cook
    gently for 10 minutes.
2   Add the artichoke hearts and cold water and cook
    for 10 more minutes. Bring to a boil, add the rice
    and cook for 20 minutes or until just tender. Stir in
    the grated Pecorino cheese to serve.

Squash Risotto

Serves 4

450 g (1 lb) squash
100 g (4 oz) butter
1 l (2 pt) boiling water
350 g (12 oz) Arborio rice
2 chicken or beef stock cubes
25 g (1 oz) grated Parmesan cheese
salt

1 Remove the seeds from the squash, then peel and cube. Place the cubed squash and half of the butter in a saucepan and fry for a minute, add a ladleful of boiling water and cook gently until half cooked. Add the rice to the squash, stir and fry for a minute; then add a ladleful of boiling water and crumble in stock cubes, stirring constantly and adding more water as each ladleful is absorbed. Continue the process until the rice is cooked. Turn off the heat, add the remaining butter and stir in the grated Parmesan cheese. Season with salt to taste and serve.

Shrimp Risotto

Serves 4
6 tbsp butter
vegetable oil
½ carrot, chopped
½ small onion, chopped
1 stick celery, chopped
about 4 tbsp brandy
pinch dried thyme
150 ml (5 fl oz) dry white wine
450 g (1 lb) uncooked shrimp,
   shelled, deveined
1½ l (3 pt) chicken stock
350 g (12 oz) Arborio rice
salt

1 Preheat the oven to 200°C/400°F/Gas Mark
   6. Heat half of the butter with 1 tbsp oil in a
   saucepan, add the chopped vegetables and
   cook until they are softened.
2 Pour in the brandy and add the thyme. Cook
   gently, stirring, until the liquid has evaporated.
   Then add the wine and reduce by half. Add the
   shrimp and cook for 15 minutes. Keep hot.
3 Bring the stock to a boil, pour in the rice and add a
   pinch of salt. Bring back to a boil, then cover and
   bake for 20 minutes. Drain the rice, fluff with a fork,
   mix in the remaining butter and pour the shrimp
   mixture over it.

Rice

Italy is Europe's biggest rice producer. Piedmont and
Lombardy are the regions where it is grown. Italian
rice has shorter, fatter grains than the Asian varieties.
It takes a little longer to cook, but has more bite and
body and is excellent for risotto and for soups where
the grains must remain firm and creamy as well as
succulent. Arborio is the variety usually exported.
Asian rice is better for timbales, salads and pilafs,
as it can be cooked until it is dry and fluffy.

Asparagus Risotto

Serves 4
450 g (1 lb) asparagus
vegetable oil
6 tbsp chopped bacon
1 onion, chopped
1 clove garlic, chopped
1 bunch parsley, chopped
salt
250 g (9 oz) Arborio rice
50 g (2 oz) diced Caciocavallo cheese

1 Clean the asparagus, cut off tough stalk ends and
   boil for 12 minutes in salted water. Drain, reserving
   the cooking liquid; cut off asparagus tips.
2 In a saucepan, heat the oil and fry the bacon,
   onion, garlic and parsley. Pour on a little
   asparagus liquid, season with salt and bring to
   a boil.
3 Add the rice, adding more asparagus liquid as it
   is absorbed. When the rice is cooked, mix in the
   diced Caciocavallo cheese and asparagus tips.

Rice with Broad Beans

Serves 4

3 strips bacon
1 onion
1 clove garlic
½ stick celery
1 bunch parsley
vegetable oil
2 medium tomatoes, peeled, chopped, and
    crushed with a fork
salt and freshly ground black pepper
350 g (12 oz) shelled fresh broad beans
350 g (12 oz) Arborio rice
grated Pecorino cheese

1 Chop the bacon, onion, garlic, celery and parsley
   finely together. Heat a little oil in a saucepan and
   cook the mixture gently, stirring.
2 Add the prepared tomatoes, season with salt and
   pepper and cook for 10 minutes. Add the broad
   beans and 1½ l (3 pt) water. Bring to a boil and
   add the rice. Cook for 20 minutes or until the rice is
   done and the consistency is thick and soupy
3 Sprinkle with Pecorino to serve.

Sardinian Risotto with Tomato Sauce

Serves 4

5 tbsp butter
350 g (12 oz) Arborio
    rice
salt and freshly
    ground black
    pepper
2 vegetable stock
    cubes

1 clove garlic
½ stick celery
½ small onion
1 small bunch
    parsley
450 g (1 lb) tomatoes,
    chopped
salt and freshly
    ground black
    pepper

For the sauce

65 g (2½ oz) chopped
    lean pancetta
vegetable oil

2 tbsp grated
    Pecorino cheese

1 Heat 3 tbsp butter in a saucepan, add the rice,
   season with salt and pepper and cook for a few
   minutes. Pour in 1¼ litres (2½ pt) boiling water and
   crumble in the stock cubes. Stir gently as the rice
   absorbs the water.
2 Meanwhile, prepare the sauce. Fry the pancetta
   in a little oil, remove with a slotted spoon and set
   aside. Chop the garlic, celery, onion and parsley
   together, add them to the pancetta drippings and
   lightly brown. Add the tomatoes, season with salt
   and pepper and cook for 15 minutes.
3 Finally, add the pancetta. Remove the rice from
   the heat, stir in the remaining butter and grated
   Pecorino cheese and pour the hot sauce over.

Rice with Ham and Chicken Livers

Serves 4

½ small onion, finely chopped
5 tbsp butter, diced
150 g (5 oz) diced lean pancetta
salt and freshly ground black pepper
120 ml (4 fl oz) dry Marsala or red wine
100 g (4 oz) sliced chicken livers
100 g (4 oz) julienne-cut prosciutto
350 g (12 oz) rice
chicken or beef stock
5 tbsp grated Parmesan cheese

1 Fry the onion in 2 tbsp butter, add the pancetta, season with salt and pepper and cook gently for 2 minutes. Add the Marsala or red wine and let it evaporate almost completely.
2 Stir in the livers and prosciutto. Add the rice and ladle in stock gradually as the rice absorbs it, stirring constantly.
3 Remove the risotto from the heat; stir in the remaining butter and a little Parmesan.
4 Leave to stand for 1 minute, then serve sprinkled with the remaining Parmesan.

Mussel Risotto

Serves 4

1 kg (2 lb) mussels
vegetable oil
3 cloves garlic, chopped
½ small onion, chopped
6 tbsp butter
350 g (12 oz) Arborio rice
salt and freshly ground black pepper
fish stock or salted water

1 Pull off and discard the beards from the mussels; wash them thoroughly in running water. Put them into a big saucepan with a little oil and half of the garlic and put over a gentle heat. As the mussels open, remove them from their shells and set aside. Strain the cooking liquid and reserve
2 Soften the remaining garlic and the onion in 4 tbsp butter and a little oil. Add the rice. Season with salt and freshly ground pepper, adding fish stock or salted water a ladleful at a time until the rice is tender.
3 Just before removing from the heat, stir in the mussels and strained mussel liquid; add remaining butter and serve.

PIZZA

The pizza originated in Naples, an invention of Neapolitan bakers for the poverty-stricken inhabitants of the backstreets of the city, to make a little food stretch a long way. As it is still a cheap and cheerful way to eat, the pizza has become even more popular in other countries than it is in Italy and there are pizza restaurants all over the world.

Deep-dish Mozzarella and Salami Pizza

Makes 2 x 20 cm (8 in) pizzas
225 g (8 oz) flour made into Pizza Dough
    (see page 43)
400 g (15 oz) canned tomatoes, drained
2 tsp olive oil
12 slices Italian salami
2 tbsp Parmesan cheese
1 tsp oregano
12 thin slices Mozzarella cheese
salt and freshly ground black pepper
50 g (2 oz) black olives

1 Make the dough and let rise. Knock back and shape in 2 x 20 cm (8 in) flan rings placed on a baking sheet.
2 Preheat the oven to 220°C/425°F/Gas Mark 7. Mash down the tomatoes and add a little of the drained juice. Brush the dough with oil and arrange the tomatoes on the bottom.
3 Roll the salami into rounds. Sprinkle a little Parmesan cheese on the tomato and then the oregano. Arrange the salami rolls. Place the slices of Mozzarella cheese alternately with salami. Season well. Sprinkle on the remaining Parmesan and decorate with black olives.
4 Brush over with oil and cook in a hot oven for 20 minutes. Reduce the heat to 190°C/375°F/Gas Mark 5 for 5–10 more minutes.

Pizza Fantasia

Serves 4
225 g (8 oz) flour made into Pizza Dough
    (see page 43)
350 g (12 oz) peeled, chopped tomatoes
finely diced Mozzarella cheese
8 flat anchovy fillets, chopped
12 pitted green olives
1 tbsp capers
4 small pickles
100g (4 oz) tinned artichoke hearts, drained
    and sliced
freshly ground black pepper
4 tbsp olive oil

1 Preheat the oven to 240°C/475°F/Gas Mark 9. Roll out the dough into a circle, put on an oiled baking sheet and cover with tomatoes.
2 Arrange Mozzarella, anchovies, olives, capers, pickles and artichoke hearts on top. Sprinkle with pepper and drizzle with oil.
3 Bake in the preheated oven for 15 minutes.

Mozzarella

Genuine Mozzarella cheeses come from Campania and Apulia and are made with buffalo milk. True Mozzarella is increasingly difficult to find because of the scarcity of the buffalo. The cheese commonly available today is made from cows' milk. It should be eaten absolutely fresh and moist and is sold in round balls wrapped in greaseproof paper to keep it that way. If the cheese has dried out a little, it is best used in cooking or to top pizzas.

Pizza Siciliana

Serves 2–4

225 g (8 oz) flour made into Pizza Dough
  (see page 43)
olive oil
150 ml (5 fl oz) Tomato Sauce (see page 88)
4 tomatoes, skinned and sliced
½ tsp oregano
salt and freshly ground black pepper
50 g (2 oz) Parmesan cheese
1 can anchovies
75 g (3 oz) black olives

1 Shape the dough into a rectangular shape
30 x 20 cm (12 x 18 in) or use a flan tin or a large
jelly roll pan.
2 Preheat the oven to 220°C/425°F/Gas Mark 7.
Paint the dough with a pastry brush dipped in
olive oil and then cover the surface with the tomato
sauce. Place the sliced tomatoes on top and
sprinkle with oregano and seasoning. Sprinkle
with Parmesan cheese.
3 Drain the anchovies and arrange the halved fillets
in a lattice design. Place an olive in the center of
each lattice.
4 Paint over with the remaining oil and bake for 15
minutes. Then turn the heat down to
190°C/375°F/Gas Mark 5 for 10 more minutes.

Family Pizza

Serves 4

225 g (8 oz) flour made into Pizza Dough
  (see page 43)
150 ml (5 fl oz) Tomato Sauce (see page 88)
400 g (15 oz) canned chopped tomatoes
1 green pepper
½ tsp oregano
salt and freshly ground black pepper
75 g (3 oz) grated Cheddar cheese
3 pork sausages

1 Follow the Siciliana recipe (left) as far as painting
the dough with the oil and arranging the sauce
on top. Add the chopped tomatoes. Dice the
green pepper into small pieces, blanch it for 20
minutes and drain it. Scatter the oregano and
pepper on the tomato mixture, followed by the
grated Cheddar. Cut the pork sausages in pieces
diagonally and arrange on top of the pizza. Cook
as for Pizza Siciliana.

Deep-dish Mushroom and Prosciutto Pizza

Makes 2 x 20 cm (8 in) pizzas

225 g (8 oz) whole wheat flour made into Pizza Dough (see page 43)

Topping

1 tbsp oil
400 g (15 oz) canned tomatoes, drained
4 tomatoes, skinned and sliced
1 tsp oregano
salt and freshly ground black pepper
2 tbsp Parmesan cheese
butter
350 g (12 oz) mushrooms, washed and sliced
8 thin slices smoked ham (prosciutto)

1 Shape the dough in 2 x 20 cm (8 in) flan rings placed on a baking sheet. Paint the shaped dough with a pastry brush dipped in oil.
2 Preheat the oven to 220°C/425°F/Gas Mark 7. Arrange the tomatoes on the bases of the pizza dough. Sprinkle with oregano and salt and pepper. Sprinkle half of the cheese over the tomato mixture.
3 Melt the butter and the remaining oil in a frying pan and cook the mushrooms over low heat for about 4 minutes.
4 Spread the mushrooms on top of the pizzas and arrange the ham on top. Sprinkle with the remaining cheese.
5 Bake for 15 minutes, before turning the oven down to 190°C/375°F/Gas Mark 5 for the last 10 minutes.

Whole Wheat Pepper and Caper Pizza

Makes 2 x 20 cm (8 in) pizzas

225 g (8 oz) whole wheat flour made into Pizza Dough (see page 43)

Topping

1 tbsp oil
400 g (15 oz) canned tomatoes
½ tsp fresh or ¼ tsp dried thyme
175 g (6 oz) mushrooms, washed and sliced
1 tbsp capers, chopped
salt and freshly ground black pepper
2 tbsp Parmesan cheese
1 red pepper, seeded

1 Shape the dough in 2 x 20 cm (8 in) flan rings placed on a baking sheet, and brush with oil.
2 Preheat the oven to 220°C/425°F/Gas Mark 7. Drain and chop the tomatoes, mix with the thyme and spread on the pizza bases. Arrange the mushrooms on the two bases and sprinkle with chopped capers. Season well with salt and pepper.
3 Sprinkle with grated cheese and arrange strips of red pepper on top. Bake for 15 minutes then reduce the temperature to 190°C/375°F/Gas Mark 5 for another 10 minutes.

Whole Wheat Eggplant and Mozzarella Pizza

Makes 1 x 20 cm (8 in) pizza
100 g (4 oz) whole wheat flour made into Pizza
   Dough (see page 43)
2 tbsp oil
1 small eggplant, sliced
salt and freshly ground black pepper
150 ml (5 fl oz) Tomato Sauce (see page 88)
1 small red pepper, seeded
3 stuffed olives, halved
50 g (2 oz) Mozzarella cheese

1   Shape the pizza into a 20 cm (8 in) round and rub
    a little oil over the dough.
2   Preheat the oven to 220°C/425°F/Gas Mark 7.
    Sprinkle the sliced eggplant with salt and let stand
    for a few minutes. Spread the tomato sauce over
    the dough. Cut six rings of red pepper.
3   Heat the remaining oil in the frying pan. Drain the
    eggplant slices of juice on paper towels and fry for
    about 30 seconds on each side.
4   Arrange them on the pizza with a ring of red
    pepper on top and half an olive in the center.
    Place the slices of Mozzarella between the
    eggplant slices and bake for 15 minutes. Turn the
    heat down to 190°C /375°F/Gas Mark 5 for the
    final 10 minutes of cooking.

Deep-dish Artichoke Heart and Bacon Pizza

Makes 2 x 20 cm (8 in) pizzas
225 g (8 oz) flour made into Pizza Dough
   (see page 43)
1 tbsp olive oil
300 ml (10 fl oz) Tomato Sauce 2 (see page 88)
100 g (4 oz) canned artichoke hearts, drained
12 rashers bacon
1 tbsp Parmesan cheese
1 tbsp freshly chopped basil or parsley leaves

1   Shape the risen dough into 2 x 20 cm (8 in) flan
    rings or cake pans.
2   Preheat the oven to 220°C/425°F/Gas Mark 7.
    Brush over the dough with the oil and divide the
    tomato sauce between the two bases. Drain the
    artichoke hearts. Roll up the slices of bacon and
    broil or bake for a few minutes.
3   Sprinkle the pizzas with Parmesan cheese
    and herbs. Arrange the artichoke hearts
    alternately with the bacon rolls. Brush over with
    the remaining oil.
4   Bake for 15–20 minutes before reducing the heat
    to 190°C/375°F/Gas Mark 5 for 5 more minutes.

Neapolitan Pizza

Makes 1 x 30 cm (12 in) pizza

225 g (8 oz) flour made into Pizza Dough
    (see page 43)
1 tbsp olive oil
1 clove garlic, crushed
6 tomatoes, skinned and sliced
½ tsp oregano
4 chopped basil leaves

1 Preheat the oven to 220°C/425°F/Gas Mark 7. Take the dough and roll into a round shape, kneading the round out to 30 cm (12 in) size with floured knuckles. Make sure that it is not too thick. Any leftover dough can be allowed to rise and cooked as a bread roll.

2 A large flan tin is ideal for this type of pizza but it also shapes well on a greased baking tray.

3 Brush over the dough with the olive oil and rub over the whole surface with the well crushed clove of garlic.

4 Arrange the tomatoes over the surface and sprinkle with herbs. Fresh parsley may be used if basil is unobtainable. Season well. Place in a hot oven for 20–25 minutes.

5 This is the basic tomato pizza but most people prefer to add extra toppings (see page 111).

Deep-dish Ham and Mushroom Pizza

Makes 2 x 20 cm (8 in) pizzas

225 g (8 oz) flour made into Pizza Dough (see
   page 43)
1 tbsp oil
300 ml (10 fl oz) well flavored Béchamel
Sauce (see page 85)
100 g (4 oz) mushrooms, washed and sliced
400 g (15 oz) canned tomatoes, drained
salt and freshly ground black pepper
½ tsp oregano
6 slices cooked ham
100 g (4 oz) Mozzarella cheese, thinly sliced

1 Shape the risen dough into 2 x 20 cm (8 in) flan
   tins. Preheat the oven to 220°C/425°F/Gas Mark 7.
2 Brush over the dough with oil and divide the
   Béchamel sauce between the two bases. Arrange
   half the sliced mushrooms on the Béchamel
   sauce. Chop the tomatoes and divide between the
   two bases. Season well and sprinkle with oregano.
3 Cut the slices of ham in half and roll them up,
   placing six rolls on each pizza, alternating with thin
   slices of Mozzarella cheese. Garnish with sliced
   mushrooms.
4 Bake in the oven for 15 minutes and then reduce
   the heat to 190°C/375°F/Gas Mark 5 for 10 more
   minutes.

Pizza Toppings

Toppings for Pizza Marinara
3 medium, firm and ripe tomatoes (not watery)
2–3 cloves garlic
dried oregano
olive oil
coarse salt

Toppings for Pizza Stagioni
cooked clams
cooked mussels
pitted olives cut into pieces
flat anchovy fillets
marinated artichoke hearts

Toppings for Pizza Margherita
thin slivers of Mozzarella cheese
tomatoes
grated fresh basil
grated Pecorino cheese
salt
olive oil

Other suggested toppings:
capers
black and green olives
marinated mushrooms
roasted peppers cut into strips
seafood (add near the end of cooking time)
dried tuna
sliced cooked ham
cubed salami
sliced pancetta
sliced sausage
cubed Fontina cheese
Gruyère, Gorgonzola, Gouda cheeses
   (grated or sliced)
sliced hard-boiled eggs
fresh or dried basil, marjoram, parsley

VEGETABLES

In Italy, vegetables are rarely served as an accompaniment to the meat course. Instead, vegetable dishes are often served as a separate course, presented before the meat. A visit to any Italian market will reveal the importance of vegetables in the national cuisine; the range of produce on display will most likely be local in origin and seasonal in nature. Freshness and flavor is everything to the Italian cook!

Fennel Milanese Style

Serves 4–6

3 medium fennel bulbs
150 ml (5 fl oz) white wine
2 tbsp vinegar
1 clove garlic
2 bay leaves
salt
2 eggs
175 g (6 oz) fresh breadcrumbs
150 ml (5 fl oz) olive oil

1 Fennel, though bulb-like, is also slightly flat. So cut it into 6 mm (¼ in) slices from the root upwards, in the same plane as its flat side. You will find that the inner three or four slices hang together as cross-sections of the plant. Set all these aside.

2 Put the rest, with the white wine, vinegar, garlic and bay leaves, into 900 ml (2 pt) water, and bring everything to a boil. Salt the liquid to taste and poach the fennel cross sections in it for 10–15 minutes or until soft. Drain the fennel and pat it dry.

3 In a shallow bowl, beat the two eggs well. Dip each fennel piece into the egg, covering it well. Shake off any excess. Now press the fennel slices forcefully into the breadcrumbs, spread out on a flat surface to facilitate the process.

4 Heat the oil until hot; fry each fennel slice until crisp on both sides. Eat while hot.

Cabbage with Bacon and Potatoes

Serves 6

1 head savoy cabbage (about 1 kg/2 lb)
salt and freshly ground black pepper
4 tbsp butter
175 g (6 oz) chopped smoked pancetta
chicken stock
ground nutmeg
500 g (1¼ lb) potatoes
milk
2 egg yolks

1 Preheat the oven to 180°C/350°F/Gas Mark 4. Trim the cabbage and blanch in salted water for 10 minutes. Drain and squeeze out the water, then chop coarsely.

2 Heat a little butter in a large saucepan, add the pancetta and cabbage, stir well and cover with stock. Season with salt, pepper and nutmeg and bring to a boil, then simmer over medium heat for 45 minutes.

3 Boil the potatoes in another saucepan. Peel, then press through a strainer or mash well while still hot. Put the mashed potatoes in a small saucepan over medium heat, add 4 tbsp butter and enough milk to give a soft, but not runny, consistency. Season and mix in the egg yolks.

4 Butter the baking dish, spoon in the cabbage mixture and pipe on mashed potatoes. Dot the top with the remaining butter and bake for 10 minutes. Serve hot.

Spinach with Oil, Lemon and Pepper

Serves 4–6
1 kg (2 lb) fresh spinach
150 ml (5 fl oz) olive oil
juice of ½ lemon
salt and freshly ground black pepper

1   Trim the stalks from the spinach leaves
(see Cook's tip).
2   Very lightly oil the bottom of a heavy saucepan
and set in on low heat. Introduce the spinach
a little at a time. It will shrink as it comes into
contact with the heat. Cover the saucepan and
steam the spinach for about 10 minutes over fairly
low heat.
3   When the spinach is cooked, press it lightly in a
colander and save the juices for another use (see
Cook's tip). Allow the spinach to cool slightly. Then
simply dress it with the olive oil, lemon juice, salt
and black pepper.
4   Eat it hot, warm or cool.

Fried Radicchio

Serves 4
8 heads radicchio
extra-virgin olive oil
salt and freshly ground black pepper

1   Wash the radicchio well without removing the
leaves and drain off as much water as possible.
Then cut into quarters from stem to tip and
squeeze out more excess water (otherwise the oil
will spit when heated). Put the quarters on a plate
and sprinkle with oil, salt and pepper. Put a large
frying pan on to heat and, when hot, put in the
radicchio and cook briskly, turning over as soon as
each side is cooked. Arrange on a serving dish.
This method results in crisp radicchio – for softer
radicchio, cook, covered, over lower heat.

Cook's Tip
You can make soup with the spinach stalks, as you
can with the juices of the spinach, if you go to the
trouble of keeping them for later use, either in the
fridge or in the freezer.

Baked Eggplant with Mozzarella

Serves 4

2 medium eggplant
4 tbsp olive oil
450 g (1 lb) fresh or canned plum tomatoes
2 tbsp fresh oregano (1 tbsp if using dried)
salt and freshly ground black pepper
225 g (8 oz) Mozzarella cheese
3 tbsp freshly grated Parmesan cheese

1. Preheat the oven to 200°C/400°F/Gas Mark 6. Cut off the coarse stalks of the eggplant and slice them lengthways into 1 cm (½ in) slices. Bake the slices in the oven, directly on the oven shelf, for 10 minutes or until very soft.

2. In the meantime, oil a baking dish. Chop the tomatoes roughly and combine with the oregano. Season strongly with the salt and pepper. Grate the Mozzarella and mix it with the Parmesan.

3. Remove the eggplant slices from the oven and line the baking dish with one layer. Spread the tomato and oregano mixture evenly over it, and sprinkle the Mozzarella and Parmesan on top of that. Continue to make these layers until the dish is full, leaving yourself a good amount of Mozzarella and Parmesan as a final, thick coating: the cheese will melt and seal the dish as it cooks.

4. Bake until the cheese melts and browns – about 15–20 minutes.

Zucchini Fried in Light Batter

Serves 4
450 g (1 lb) zucchini
225 g (8 oz) all-purpose flour
salt and freshly ground black pepper
300 ml (10 fl oz) vegetable oil

1 Slice the zucchini into batons approximately 1 cm (½ in) thick and 5 cm (2 in) long, depending on the size of the individual vegetables.
2 Sift the flour with the salt and pepper, then mix it very gradually with water, beating the mixture constantly to avoid lumps. Stop adding water when your batter reaches the consistency of thick cream.
3 Heat the oil until very hot, dip the zucchini in the batter, and then fry them in batches – they should fit only loosely into the saucepan so that they brown evenly. When the batter is crisp and brown, the vegetables are ready.
4 Zucchini should be served hot.

Savoy Cabbage Stuffed with Scamorza Cheese

Serves 4
1 head savoy cabbage, about 450 g (1 lb)
175 g (6 oz) thinly sliced Scamorza or Mozzarella cheese
vegetable oil
1 tbsp chopped onion
500 g (1¼ lb) tomatoes, peeled, seeded and pressed through a strainer
salt and freshly ground black pepper
few tbsp grated Parmesan cheese

1 Preheat the oven to 180°C/350°F/Gas Mark 4. Trim the cabbage stem and remove the outer leaves. Boil or steam the whole cabbage until cooked but still firm. Leave to cool.
2 Remove the leaves and divide into 8 piles. Fill the top leaf in each pile with Scamorza or Mozzarella and roll up each pile around the cheese. Heat a little oil in a frying pan and fry the onion until soft. Add the tomatoes, season with salt and pepper and cook over medium heat until very soft, being careful not to let the sauce dry out.
3 Put a layer of tomato sauce in a baking dish, arrange cabbage rolls on top and pour the remaining sauce over. Sprinkle with Parmesan, bake for 10 minutes and serve while piping hot.

Eggplant Baked with Garlic Sott'olio

> **Serves 4–6**
> 2 large eggplant
> 4 cloves garlic
> 150 ml (5 fl oz) olive oil
> juice of ½ lemon
> salt and freshly ground black pepper

1 Preheat the oven to 200°C/400°F/Gas Mark 6. Cut the spiky stalk off the eggplant. Peel the garlic cloves and cut them lengthways into thinnish slivers.
2 Pierce the eggplant all over with a thin-bladed knife. Push the slivers of garlic into the slits.
3 Place the eggplant directly onto the oven shelf. Do not oil them in any way. Bake for 15 minutes, until the vegetables shrink and the skins wrinkle. When cooked, they will feel soft to the touch.
4 Remove the eggplant from the oven and let stand for 3–4 minutes.
5 Slice them into neat, thin, strips lengthways. Dress them with the oil, lemon juice, salt and pepper. Serve the eggplant hot, warm or cool.

Broccoli with Green Pepper and Garlic

> **Serves 4–6**
> salt
> 675 g (1½ lb) fresh broccoli
> 30 ml (1 fl oz) olive oil
> 1 small green pepper, seeded and finely sliced
> 4 cloves garlic, crushed
> ¾ tbsp freshly grated Parmesan cheese
> freshly ground black pepper

1 Bring plenty of salted water to a boil. Drop in the trimmed broccoli florets and boil for 3 minutes. Drain them and stop the cooking process by plunging them immediately into cold water.
2 Heat the olive oil over high heat. Cook the pepper in the oil until the slices begin to brown slightly at the edges. Reduce the heat to a simmer and add the garlic. Cook the pepper and garlic together for 1–2 minutes.
3 Add the broccoli and the grated Parmesan cheese turn in the oil and Parmesan until the broccoli is hot.
4 Serve immediately, lavishly sprinkled with pepper.

Gratinéed Artichokes

Serves 4–6
450 g (1 lb) artichokes
salt
4 tbsp butter
3 tbsp freshly grated Parmesan cheese
freshly ground black pepper

1   Preheat the oven to 200°C/400°F/Gas Mark 6. Vigorously scrub the artichokes and cut away any darker patches of skin. (There is no need to peel them).
2   Drop the artichokes in boiling salted water – cover well – and cook for 10 minutes. The hearts should be firm but easy to bite into. Drain.
3   Grease a baking dish with a little of the butter and place the artichokes. Dot the rest of the butter over the top.
4   Sprinkle with the Parmesan and plenty of pepper. Bake until the cheese and butter form an enticing brown crust. Serve very hot.

Artichokes

The artichoke is an edible thistle and has had a place of honor in kitchen gardens since the Renaissance. The Italians have a huge variety of artichoke recipes, including some for young artichokes eaten whole.

Soak artichokes upside down in a bowl of cold water with vinegar or lemon juice. Cut off the stem near the base of the vegetable and cut the tips cleanly off the leaves. Rub any cut edges with lemon juice.

Bring a large saucepan of salted, water with vinegar or lemon juice to a boil. Put the artichokes in, stem down, bring back to the boil and test after 30 minutes to see if they are done. Tug at a leaf at the base of the largest artichoke – if it comes away easily, the artichokes are done. Drain them upside down in a colander, and serve with a sauce.

To eat, pull away the leaves, beginning at the base. Dip the succulent base of the leaf in the sauce provided and nibble away the fleshy part. When all the leaves have been removed, discard the choke. Eat the delicious heart of the artichoke with a knife and fork and more of the sauce. To prepare artichokes for stuffing, slice off the top as well as the stem before you boil it. When it is cooked, remove the inner leaves and the choke so that you are left with a cup. If only the heart is needed, cook the artichokes in the usual way. Dismantle each artichoke, as if you were eating it, to uncover the heart.

Artichoke Hearts with Spinach

Serves 4
8 artichoke hearts
juice of 1 lemon
olive oil
all-purpose flour
500 g (1¼ lb) fresh spinach
3 tbsp butter
salt and freshly ground black pepper
1 tbsp grated Parmesan cheese

For the sauce
50 g (2 oz) butter
2 tbsp all-purpose flour
150 ml (5 fl oz) milk
150 ml (5 fl oz) whipping cream
salt and freshly ground black pepper
ground nutmeg
25 g (1 oz) grated Swiss cheese

To assemble
2 tbsp grated Parmesan cheese
3 tbsp breadcrumbs
1 tbsp butter

1 Preheat the oven to 190°C/375°F/Gas Mark 5. Steam or boil the artichoke hearts in water with lemon juice, to which you have added 1 tbsp oil and 1 tsp flour.

2 Meanwhile, trim and wash the spinach in several changes of water, then boil in the water clinging to the leaves. When cooked, rinse in cold water and squeeze dry.

3 Melt 3 tbsp butter in a saucepan, add the spinach, season with salt and pepper and cook over low heat until butter is absorbed. Then stir in 1 tbsp Parmesan.

4 For the sauce, melt 50 g (2 oz) butter in a small saucepan and add the flour, blending well with a wooden spoon to avoid lumps. Add the milk and cream, season with salt, pepper and nutmeg and cook, stirring, until the sauce has thickened and is simmering. Stir in the cheese and remove from the heat.

5 To assemble, grease a large baking dish. Cut a thin slice off the bottom of the artichoke hearts so that they stand upright and arrange them in a dish. Divide the spinach between them, molding equally on top, pour over the sauce, sprinkle with 2 tbsp Parmesan and breadcrumbs and dot with 1 tbsp butter. Bake for 10 minutes or until golden. Serve immediately.

Asparagus with Eggs and Cheese

Serves 4
1½ kg (3 lb) asparagus
4 eggs
6 tbsp butter
3 tbsp grated Parmesan cheese

1 Clean the asparagus and cut off tough stalk ends before boiling or steaming. Drain and arrange on a heated serving dish. Fry the eggs in about 4 tbsp butter until just set. Heat the remaining butter separately. Sprinkle the Parmesan on the asparagus, put the eggs carefully on top, then drizzle with melted butter. Serve piping hot.

Beets with Cream and Mushrooms

Serves 4
5 tbsp butter
vegetable oil
175 g (6 oz) sliced fresh mushrooms
1 clove garlic, chopped
1½ kg (3 lb) beets, cooked, peeled, chopped
2 eggs
3 tbsp whipping cream
1½ tbsp grated Parmesan cheese
salt and freshly ground black pepper
breadcrumbs

1 Preheat the oven to 350°F/180°C/Gas Mark 4. Melt the butter with a little oil in a frying pan, add the mushrooms and garlic and fry until soft. Stir in the beets and cook gently so that the flavors mingle. Put the eggs in a bowl with the cream and Parmesan and beat together well. Season with salt and pepper. Add the beets mixture and stir well to coat in egg mixture. Grease a baking dish, sprinkle with breadcrumbs and fill with beets mixture, leveling off the top. Sprinkle with breadcrumbs again, drizzle a little oil over the top and bake until golden.

Mushrooms Trifolare

Serves 6

675 g (1½ lb) good mushrooms (see Cook's tip)
4 tbsp olive oil
3 cloves garlic, crushed
2 heaped tbsp chopped fresh parsley
salt and freshly ground black pepper

1 Wash but do not peel – never peel – the mushrooms. Slice or chop them into thumb-sized chunks if they are particularly large.

2 Heat the oil to medium and sauté the crushed garlic for about 30 seconds. Add the mushrooms. These will absorb the oil very promptly. When they do, turn down the heat and wait for the process to reverse – the mushrooms begin to give off their own liquid. This will take 2 minutes or so.

3 Increase the heat and add the parsley, salt and pepper. Cook for 2–3 more minutes.

Spinach, Roman Style

Serves 4

1 kg (2 lb) fresh spinach
vegetable oil
1 clove garlic, crushed
65 g (2½ oz) finely diced bacon
3 tbsp pine nuts
3 tbsp golden raisins, soaked in lukewarm water
    until plump
salt
butter

1 Wash the spinach, discarding any tough stalks or discolored leaves. Cook gently in the water clinging to leaves, then drain and squeeze dry

2 Heat a little oil in a saucepan, add garlic, bacon and spinach, and cook, gently stirring. After a few minutes, add the pine nuts and raisins. Remove from the heat, season with salt, put in a serving dish, top with about 1 tbsp butter and serve.

Cook's Tip
The Italian verb "to fry with garlic and parsley" is *trifolare* and you will find quite a number of things *trifolati* – zucchini for example.

FISH

As the Italians are firm believers in using only fresh local produce, you will be unlikely to find seafood in Italy at any distance from the coast. Fish – whether from the sea or rivers – is perhaps at its best simply cooked with butter or olive oil, plus a few sage leaves, and served with a wedge of lemon.

Trout al Carpione

Serves 6

6 medium rainbow trout or 1 salmon,
    about 1½ kg (3¼ lb)
1 egg
300 ml (10 fl oz) olive oil
100 g (4 oz) all-purpose flour
1 large onion
4 cloves of garlic
150 ml (5 fl oz) dry white wine
2 tbsp vinegar
2 tbsp sugar
2 large sprigs rosemary
4 fresh bay leaves
1 chili
salt

1 Clean and dry the fish. If you are using salmon, cut it into slices about 1 cm (½ in) thick.
2 Beat the egg and mix with its own volume of water. Heat about one-third of the oil to a medium heat, dip the whole fish or slices in the egg/water mixture and then roll in the flour. Fry gently until cooked – whole trout 8 minutes per side, slices 4–5 minutes. When cooking fish in this way, always turn it only once.
3 Carefully remove the fish when it is cooked and arrange it attractively on a serving dish.
4 Set the rest of the olive oil on medium heat. Slice the onion very finely and stew it in the oil (stew, not fry!). Add the garlic and cook both together until the onion is completely soft. Do not brown.
5 Add the wine, vinegar, sugar, rosemary, bay leaves and the whole chili. Bring everything to a boil and season. Pour the mixture over the fish and serve either warm, cool or chilled.

Fried Stuffed Sardines

Serves 4

16 fresh sardines
olive oil
2 tbsp dried mushrooms, soaked and drained
1 tbsp fresh breadcrumbs, softened in a little milk
    and squeezed dry
1 tbsp grated Parmesan cheese
1 clove garlic, crushed
1 tsp chopped fresh marjoram
pinch dried oregano
4 eggs
salt and freshly ground back pepper
all-purpose flour
fine dry breadcrumbs

1 Clean the sardines, removing the heads and tails. Open them out, remove the bones, wash and pat dry. Heat a little olive oil in a frying pan, chop the mushrooms finely and fry gently for a few minutes. Transfer them to a dish and add fresh breadcrumbs, Parmesan, garlic, marjoram, oregano, two eggs and a pinch of salt.
2 Stuff the sardines with this mixture, then close them up. Beat the remaining two eggs with salt and pepper. Dip the stuffed sardines first into flour, then into seasoned beaten egg, then into dry breadcrumbs. Fry in hot oil and serve immediately.

Brochettes of Monkfish with Basil and Orange

Serves 4
1 kg (2 lb) monkfish
2 oranges
150 ml (5 fl oz) olive oil
1 tbsp finely chopped fresh basil
25 g (1 oz) fresh breadcrumbs
salt and freshly ground black pepper

1 Skin the monkfish and dice it into 5 cm (2 in) square chunks.
2 Squeeze the juice from the oranges. Cut the rinds into chunks about the size of the monkfish pieces and reserve. Combine the olive oil, orange juice and basil.
3 Add the fish to the marinate and scatter with the pieces of orange rind. Marinate for up to 2 hours.
4 Preheat the broiler. Thread the fish onto skewers, alternating the pieces whenever you can with pieces of orange rind.
5 Brush liberally with the marinade once more. Sprinkle half of the breadcrumbs on top. Broil for 6–7 minutes. Turn, breadcrumb the other side, and broil again. Remove the brochettes to a serving platter.
6 Combine any pan juices with the rest of the marinade. Bring to a rapid boil, season and pour over the fish.

Fried Squid

Serves 6
scant 2 kg (4½ lb) small squid
600 ml (1 pt) vegetable oil
175 g (6 oz) all-purpose flour
salt and freshly ground black pepper
3 lemons, cut into wedges

1 Clean the squid. Slice the body sacs into rings – 5 or 6 per body for small squid.
2 Heat the oil until it is almost smoking. Fry the squid in batches small enough not to produce a serious drop in the oil temperature. Start with 2 or 3 and slowly work up.
3 Dip the squid in the flour, one batch at a time so the coating does not become soggy, shake off the excess and fry until light brown – about 30–40 seconds if the temperature is right. Drain on paper towels.
4 Check for salt once more when all is cooked and serve very hot, with the lemon wedges.

Skate with Anchovy Butter

Serves 4
1 kg (2 lb) skate
2 small carrots, chopped
1 stick celery, chopped
2 small onions, chopped
5 tbsp butter
25 g (1 oz) all-purpose flour
salt and freshly ground black pepper
1 tbsp capers
1 tbsp sliced gherkin
1 tbsp chopped parsley
squeeze of lemon juice
5 flat anchovy fillets soaked in milk

1 Poach the skate in a stock made from 750 ml (1½ pt) water, the carrots, celery and onions. When the fish is cooked, transfer to a serving platter and keep warm.
2 Melt 2½ tbsp butter, blend in the flour and a little fish poaching liquid. Season with salt and pepper and simmer, stirring, for 7–8 minutes until the sauce has thickened and is smooth and velvety. Add the capers, sliced gherkin, parsley and lemon juice.
3 Drain the anchovies and pound with the remaining butter. Blend the anchovy butter into the sauce. Heat through, pour over the skate and serve.

Dried Sicilian Cod

Serves 4
750 g (1½ lb) dried cod
olive oil
1 small onion, chopped
1 large clove garlic, chopped
120 ml (4 fl oz) white wine
500 g (1¼ lb) tomatoes, peeled, seeded and pressed through a strainer
salt and freshly ground black pepper
100 g (4 oz) pitted black olives
1½ tbsp capers
1 tbsp golden raisins, soaked in lukewarm water until plump
1 tbsp pine nuts
3 medium potatoes, peeled and sliced

1 Preheat the oven to 190°C/375°F/Gas Mark 5. Remove the bones and skin from the cod and cut the flesh into cubes. Heat some oil in an ovenproof saucepan, fry the onion and garlic and add the fish. Cook for a minute, then add the wine.
2 When the wine has almost evaporated, add the tomatoes and enough water to cover the fish. Season with salt and pepper. Bring to a boil, cover and bake for an hour. Add the olives, capers, raisins, pine nuts and potatoes. Continue to bake until the potatoes are done; serve immediately.

Braised Swordfish with Peppers

Serves 4
4 swordfish steaks – about 175 g (6 oz each)
4 tbsp olive oil
4 cloves garlic
1 medium onion, roughly chopped
1 medium red pepper
100 g (4 oz) fresh or canned plum tomatoes, roughly chopped
1 chili
150 ml (5 fl oz) dry white wine
salt and freshly ground black pepper

1 Wash and thoroughly dry the fish. Heat the oil over high heat and seal each steak on each side.
2 Remove the fish from the saucepan. Reduce the heat to medium and add the whole cloves of garlic and the onions.
3 Turn the heat once more to high and cook the onions until the edges begin to brown.
4 Reduce the heat to a gentle simmer and cook until the onions and garlic are softened. In the meantime, de-seed and finely slice the peppers.
5 When the onions are soft, add the peppers and cook until they begin to soften – about 5 minutes. Add the tomatoes, the whole chili and the wine. Bring to a fierce boil, then add the fish. Turn the heat to a low simmer and cover. Simmer until the fish is very tender – about 15 minutes.
6 Remove the fish from the saucepan and set it aside in a warm place. Boil the saucepan juices very briskly, until they are reduced to a thick, creamy mixture. Season, pour around the fish and serve.

Baked Stuffed Sardines

Serves 4
16 fresh sardines
2 tbsp vinegar
salt and pepper
75 g (3 oz) mixed chopped garlic, chopped parsley and grated Parmesan cheese
all-purpose flour
2 eggs, beaten
breadcrumbs
olive oil
lemon wedges

1 Preheat the oven to 190°C/375°F/Gas Mark 5. Clean the sardines, removing the heads and tails, open them out and remove the bones. Wash and pat dry. Arrange on a big dish, sprinkle with vinegar, salt and pepper and stuff each one with the garlic, parsley and cheese mixture.
2 Close the fish up again, pressing down well; dip them first in flour, next in beaten egg and then in breadcrumbs. Put the sardines on a greased baking dish, sprinkle with oil and bake for 25–30 minutes. Serve with lemon wedges.

Salad of Broiled Tuna and Bacon

Serves 4
1 kg (2 lb) fresh tuna
450 g (1 lb) bacon or pancetta
4 tbsp fresh oregano
150 ml (5 fl oz) olive oil
juice of 1 lemon
2 cloves garlic, well crushed
salt and freshly ground black pepper
1½ tbsp freshly grated Parmesan cheese

1 Dice the tuna into thumb-sized chunks. Lay the bacon out in flat strips and spread it with the oregano, very finely chopped.
2 Lay a piece of tuna at the start of each bacon strip, roll in the bacon and pin with a cocktail stick. Continue until all the tuna is wrapped.
3 Combine the olive oil and lemon juice and add the garlic. Marinate the pinned pieces of tuna and bacon in the mixture for about 2 hours.
4 Preheat the oven to broil. Thread the bacon and fish chunks onto skewers. Imagine the skewers have four sides. Grill each side for 2 minutes – four quarter turns.
5 Remove the fish from the skewers when cooked, then separate the fish and bacon. Finely chop the bacon pieces.
6 Dress the fish in the marinade, season and sprinkle the bacon and Parmesan over the top. Serve warmish.

Cook's Tip
This dish is wonderful with the bitter taste of radicchio. Shred two heads and serve the salad on top.

Braised Squid with a Parsley Stuffing

Serves 6
12 squid (about 8 cm/3¼ in long)
2 tbsp finely chopped fresh parsley
2 cloves garlic, crushed
25 g (1 oz) fresh breadcrumbs
2 anchovy fillets
1 egg
6 tbsp olive oil
225 g (8 oz) fresh or canned plum tomatoes
150 ml (5 fl oz) dry white wine
1 chili
salt and freshly ground black pepper

1 Clean the squid and finely chop the tentacles. Combine the parsley, garlic and breadcrumbs. Mash and mix in the anchovies.
2 Beat the egg and mix it with the bread mixture. Add about half of the oil and the tentacles of the squid. Now push the mixture into the squid bodies, stopping about two-thirds of the way down. (The squid will shrink as it cooks and push the stuffing down to the end).
3 Heat the rest of the oil in a saucepan large enough to hold all the fish in one layer. Roughly chop the tomatoes and add them to the oil with the wine and the whole chili.
4 Bring the tomatoes and wine to a boil, then turn the heat to a very low simmer. Add the squid and seal the saucepan tightly. Cook for about 30 minutes, until a fork will easily pierce the squid. Season the sauce with salt and pepper and wait, if you like – this dish may be served hot, cold or warm.

Red Mullet with Prosciutto

Serves 4
12 small red mullet
salt
12 slices prosciutto
4 ripe tomatoes
1 clove garlic
olive oil
25 g (1 oz) breadcrumbs
freshly ground black pepper
1 tbsp chopped parsley
juice of ½ lemon

1 Clean and de-scale the fish; wash, pat dry and season with salt. Wrap each fish in a slice of prosciutto. Peel the tomatoes, then de-seed and slice them.

2 Cook the garlic for 5 minutes in a saucepan with some oil. Add the mullet and cook for 2–3 minutes on each side, turning them over gently.

3 Add the tomatoes, sprinkle with breadcrumbs, season with salt and pepper and cook over low heat for 10 minutes. Sprinkle with parsley and lemon juice. Put the mullet on a dish and serve.

Red Mullet, Livorno Style

Serves 4
450 g (1 lb) ripe tomatoes
2 tbsp butter
olive oil
few fresh basil leaves, chopped
salt and freshly ground black pepper
4 red mullets
1 stick celery
1 clove garlic
4 tbsp chopped parsley
all-purpose flour

1 Wash the tomatoes, peel and press through a strainer. In a small saucepan, heat the butter, 2 tbsp oil and the basil, then add the tomatoes, season with salt and pepper and cook gently for 30 minutes.
2 Meanwhile, clean and de-scale the fish and remove the fins; wash the fish and pat dry. Finely chop the celery and garlic. Place the celery, garlic, parsley and about 4 tbsp oil into a saucepan that you can bring to the table. Fry for a few minutes.
3 Lightly flour the fish and brown on one side. Remove from the heat and very carefully (mullets are fragile) turn them over. Put them back on the heat. Pour over the tomato sauce and cook for about 10 minutes. Serve the fish in the saucepan.

Cook's Tip
De-scaling can be a messy process. Flakes fly everywhere. Therefore, if you can, hold the fish underwater as you scrape. Hold the knife at right angles to the fish and scrape from tail to head to dislodge the scales. To clean a fish, make a single cut along the belly to the mouth. Push your hand up into the head, close your fingers firmly and pull. Everything from the lungs down will come away, cleanly. Wash away all traces of blood and proceed.

Salmon Stuffed with Black Olives

Serves 6
1 small salmon or large trout – about
  2 kg (4½ lb)
225 g (8 oz) fresh or canned plum tomatoes
4 tbsp olive oil
4 cloves garlic
2 sprigs fresh rosemary
6 anchovy fillets
25 g (1 oz) black olives
2 tbsp white wine vinegar
4 tbsp dry white wine
2 tbsp brandy
salt and freshly ground black pepper

1 Preheat the oven to 180°C/350°F/Gas Mark 4. Clean and de-scale the fish.
2 Roughly chop the tomatoes and spread them out on a large sheet of foil. Mix the olive oil with the tomatoes and lay the fish on top.
3 Crush the garlic and smear the inside of the fish with it; lay the sprigs of rosemary and the anchovy fillets at equal intervals inside the cavity. Chop the olives very finely and sprinkle half inside, half outside.
4 Combine the wine vinegar, wine and brandy and pour over the fish, then lift the sides of the foil and seal the fish carefully. Bake for 35 minutes.
5 Lift the fish from the foil with a long fish slice when it is cooked. Be careful when transferring it so that it does not break, and set it on a serving dish.
6 Pour all the juices from the foil into a saucepan and bring them to a rapid boil. Season with salt and pepper, pour over the fish and serve immediately.

Baked Sea Bass with Mayonnaise

Serves 6
1 sea bass, about 1¼ kg (3½ lb)
2 large onions
4 tbsp olive oil
2 cloves garlic
2 sprigs rosemary
2 tbsp finely chopped fresh parsley
2 tbsp finely chopped fresh basil
juice of 1 lemon
4 tbsp dry white wine
600 ml (1 pt) Mayonnaise (see page 85.)

1 Preheat the oven to 180°C/350°F/Gas Mark 4. Clean and de-scale the fish.
2 Very finely slice the onion and make a fish-shaped bed of it on a large piece of foil. Pour the olive oil over it and lay the sea bass on top.
3 Now crush the garlic and smear it along the inside of the fish. Lay the sprigs of rosemary in there too. Chop the parsley and basil finely, mix with the lemon juice, and place inside the fish.
4 Raise the edges of the foil, pour over the white wine and season. Seal the package carefully, making absolutely sure there are no holes or tears.
5 Set the package in an ample-sized dish and bake for 30 minutes. When ready, remove from the oven, but do not unseal until completely cool. In the meantime, make the mayonnaise.
6 About 45 minutes before eating, remove the fish from its wrapper and collect all the juices into a small saucepan and reserve the onions. Boil them down and leave to cool, then add them to the mayonnaise.
7 Decorate the fish with the onions and serve.

Italian Grilled Fish

Serves 4
6 whole fish – about 350 g (12 oz) each
150 ml (5 fl oz) olive oil
juice of 1 lemon
freshly ground black pepper
2 tbsp fresh oregano
1 tbsp very fine breadcrumbs
salt

1 Clean, dry and de-scale the fish, if necessary. Combine the oil and lemon juice and coat the fish thoroughly.
2 Combine the pepper, oregano, breadcrumbs and salt and rub into the fish. Leave for about 2 hours.
3 Broil the fish, turning only once.

POULTRY AND GAME

For Italians who live in the countryside, or in the south, poultry and game are virtually free foods. Many families have chickens scratching about in their backyards, and hunting is a national pastime, be it for pheasant, quail, rabbit, hare or even wild boar.

Chicken Braised with Bacon and Red Peppers

Serves 4
1¼ kg (2½ –3 lb) chicken
4 tbsp olive oil
4 red peppers
4 cloves garlic
4 chilies
225 g (½ lb) bacon or pancetta
salt

1 Joint the chicken into four pieces. Heat the oil in your heaviest casserole dish – one with a good lid – and thoroughly brown the chicken pieces. Remove the chicken from the pan.

2 Seed the red peppers and slice into fine strips. Cook until soft in the chicken oil – about 10 minutes. Return the chicken pieces to the saucepan, smothering them with the sliced peppers.

3 Add the whole garlic cloves and the whole chilies. Lay the strips of bacon over everything, cover the saucepan and cook on very low heat until the chicken is tender – about 30 minutes.

4 Season lightly with the salt. (Remember that since the bacon is salty you will only need a little).

Cook's Tip
This dish is remarkably easy to spoil. The whole point of it is that the chicken cooks in its own juices, flavored simply by the peppers. No onion. No other stock. The bacon on top provides the required lubrication. Splendid.

Italian Roast Chicken with Rosemary

Serves 4
1¼ kg (2½–3 lb) chicken
4 cloves garlic
4 good sprigs fresh rosemary
100 g (4 oz) Tritto (see page 138)
4 tbsp olive oil
4 tbsp dry white wine
salt

1 Preheat the oven to 190°C/375°F/Gas Mark 5. Put the chicken in a roasting pan, crush the garlic roughly and smear it around the cavity of the chicken, put 2 sprigs of rosemary inside, then chop the remainder and sprinkle it over and around the bird with the Tritto and oil. Put the chicken in the oven.

2 The chicken will be cooked in an hour or so, but baste it thoroughly every 15 minutes.

3 When cooking is complete, let the bird rest for 5 minutes or so. Skim the oil off the juices and set the pan over a very high heat. Add the wine and bring to a rapid boil. Season with salt, pour over the chicken and serve.

Italian Grilled Chicken

Serves 4

1 x 1¼ kg (2½–3 lb) chicken
juice of 2 lemons
150 ml (5 fl oz) olive oil
1 heaped tbsp peppercorns
kosher salt

1 Using a large pair of scissors cut out the chicken's backbone. Lay the bird breast side up on your worktop and press down onto the breast to flatten it. Now cut diagonal slashes across the breasts and thighs.

2 Set the chicken in a dish and pour the lemon juice and olive oil over it. Very roughly crush the peppercorns and sprinkle them over the chicken. Let it marinate for about two hours.

3 Preheat the oven to broil – It should be as hot as possible. Sprinkle the chicken breasts liberally with the salt. Grill until the breasts turn light brown. Turn the chicken over. Pour some of the marinade into the cavity and cook for 10 minutes.

4 Turn once more, baste with the marinade (scoop up the juices from the pan too), and remove when the whole bird is cooked and an appetizing golden brown.

Chicken Stuffed with Artichokes

Serves 4
1 clove garlic
sprig of rosemary
2 tbsp butter
salt and freshly ground black pepper
1½ kg (3 lb) chicken
4 tinned artichoke hearts
1 lemon, pierced in several places
4 fresh sage leaves
2 tbsp olive oil
about 200 ml (7 fl oz) dry white wine

1 Preheat the oven to 180°C/350°F/Gas Mark 4. Crush the garlic and rosemary. Put in a bowl with the butter, salt and pepper; mix with a wooden spoon until finely creamed.

2 Wash the chicken, pat dry and stuff with artichokes and lemon. Sew up the opening with cooking thread. Thread the chicken onto a thin skewer, putting a sage leaf under each wing and each leg. Rub the butter mixture all over the chicken, then sprinkle with salt and pepper. Put in a baking dish and pour over olive oil. Roast for 1½ hours, turning frequently.

3 Remove from the oven when golden brown. Transfer to a serving plate and cut into pieces. Arrange the artichoke hearts around the chicken. Discard the lemon. Pour the wine into the dish and warm over low heat, stirring to blend wine and juices. Pour the sauce over the chicken and serve hot.

Chicken and Rice Salad

Serves 4
200 g (7 oz) cold cooked rice
100 g (4 oz) sliced cooked chicken
100 g (4 oz) diced cooked tongue
6 tbsp slivered truffle (optional)
1 tbsp coarsely chopped fresh basil
few tomatoes, sliced
small lettuce leaves
about 3 tbsp vegetable oil
juice of 1 lemon
3 tbsp whipping cream
salt and pepper

1 Mix the rice, chicken, tongue and truffle (if using) together in a bowl. Sprinkle with basil and decorate the edges with tomatoes and lettuce. Make the dressing by mixing together the oil, lemon juice and cream; season with salt and pepper. Pour over the salad.

Pheasant Braised with Three Alcohols

Serves 4

2 pheasants
4 tbsp olive oil
1 medium onion, finely sliced
2 cloves garlic
8 sprigs of fresh rosemary
4 tbsp Marsala
4 tbsp brandy
150 ml (5 fl oz) dry white wine
salt and freshly ground black pepper

1 Preheat the oven to 170°C/325°F/Gas Mark 3. Cut away the backbones, then slice each bird in half: cut through the center of the breastbone.

2 In a pan large enough to hold the halves side by side, heat the oil. Add the finely sliced onion and whole garlic cloves.

3 As the onion cooks, flatten out the pheasants as much as you can, either with the palm of your hand or with the flat of a cleaver.

4 Lay the sprigs of rosemary on top of the softened onions, then lay the pheasant breasts down on top of that. Cook for 2–3 minutes over high heat.

5 Take a fork and liberally prick the upper, uncooked sides of the birds. Mix the Marsala and brandy together and pour an equal amount over each bird. Cover the dish very tightly and place in the oven.

6 After 1½ hours of cooking, turn the birds, scooping all the onion and rosemary you can onto the tops of the breasts. Now add the white wine.

7 Return once more to the oven and continue cooking until the pheasants are very tender – about 1 more hour. Season the juices at the last minute and pour over of the birds.

Rabbit with Onions

Serves 4

1 large rabbit – weighing about 1 kg (2 lb)
4 tbsp olive oil
3 large onions
6 cloves garlic
6 bay leaves
3 chilies
4 good sprigs fresh rosemary
4 tbsp brandy
salt and freshly ground black pepper

1 Preheat the oven to 180°C/350°F/Gas Mark 4. Cut the legs away from the rabbit carcass and cut each one once more at the knee. Cut the saddle into four pieces: haunch, belly and ribcage, split in half along the breastbone.

2 Heat the oil over medium heat and brown the rabbit pieces for 3–4 minutes. Remove them from the pan with a slotted spoon and set aside.

3 Slice the onions very finely and add them to the pan. Increase the heat and cook them until they begin to color. Reduce the heat and add the whole garlic, the whole chilies and the whole sprigs of rosemary.

4 Return the rabbit to the pan and smother with the onions. Cover tightly and put in the oven.

5 After about 1 hour, completely turn all the contents, add the brandy and season. Continue cooking until the rabbit is very tender – another 30 minutes or so.

Tritto

1 medium onion
1 carrot
1 clove garlic
½ stick celery
1 bay leaf
1 sprig rosemary
6 fresh sage leaves
enough olive oil to cover when the ingredients
   are packed

1 Very finely dice all the ingredients into 3 mm
   (⅛ in) pieces (or use a food grinder or processor).
   Sieve the pieces together so they are thoroughly
   mixed.
2 Cover with olive oil. Try not to use for at least
   12 hours. (The tritto should be packed quite tightly).

Cook's Tip

This is a pungent, well seasoned mixture of
vegetables preserved in olive oil, which absorbs
the tastes of the ingredients and then permeates
and lubricates the meat. Kept sealed and
reasonably cool, it will keep indefinitely.

   How much you make at any time will really
depend on the size of your storage jar, which
should have a spring-loaded or screw top. Make
as much as possible: you will soon find yourself
using it for roasts of all descriptions, not just Italian
ones.

   Ample instruction is given in the recipes on
the use of tritto, but the general principle is this:
any time you roast or pot roast meat – and
sometimes even fish – spread the tritto over and
around the joint. What the tiny, herb-steeped and
caramelized vegetables do to the saucepan juices
is amazing. The ingredients listed demonstrate
the proportions.

Roast Pheasant with Grapes and Walnuts

Serves 4
1 pheasant
4 strips pancetta
1 kg (2 lb) white grapes
about 250 ml (8 fl oz) sour cream
12 walnuts, shelled
2 tbsp brandy
salt and freshly ground black pepper
2 tbsp butter

1 Wrap the pheasant in pancetta and secure with
   a thin skewer. Set aside a quarter of the grapes
   and press the rest through a strainer or purée in a
   blender. Drain off and reserve the juice.
2 Put the pheasant in a saucepan; add the sour
   cream, walnuts, brandy, grape juice and a pinch
   of salt and pepper. Cover and cook over low heat
   for an hour, stirring frequently.
3 Preheat the oven to 240°C/475°F/Gas Mark 9.
   Remove the pheasant from the saucepan and take
   off the pancetta slices. Line a roasting pan with foil
   and put the pheasant in it. Roast for 10 minutes or
   until golden brown.
4 Meanwhile, remove the walnuts from the
   pheasant simmering liquid and set aside. Boil the
   liquid over high heat until reduced to 120 ml
   (4 fl oz). Add the butter and stir until it melts. Put
   the pheasant on a serving dish and surround with
   the walnuts and reserved grapes. Pour the boiling
   sauce over the pheasant and serve.

Rolled and Pot-roasted Hare

Serves 6–7

1 large hare

225 g (8 oz) unsmoked bacon or pancetta, the fattier the better

2 cloves garlic

1 heaped tbsp crushed fresh rosemary (half the quantity, if using dried)

1 heaped tbsp crushed fresh thyme (half the quantity, if using dried)

1 heaped tbsp crumbled fresh sage (half the quantity, if using dried)

4 tbsp olive oil

juice of 1 lemon

225 g (8 oz) Tritto (see page 138)

225 g (8 oz) fresh or canned plum tomatoes

300 ml (10 fl oz) dry white wine

salt and freshly ground black pepper

1 Preheat the oven to 180°C/350°F/Gas Mark 4. Remove the hare's legs. Cut through the meat along the line of the bones and remove the bones. Set them aside. Batten each of the legs into an escalope about 1 cm (½ in) thick.

2 When all four leg escalopes are nicely flat, arrange them together, with their adjoining edges overlapping slightly, so they form a rough rectangle. (You are going to lay strips of meat along the longer edge of this rectangle and then roll it up).

3 Running along the back of the hare – the saddle – are two thin, round strips of meat (the sirloins) stretching from the shoulder blades to the haunch. Run the point of a sharp knife along the top of the saddle, very close to the spine, from front to rear. This will free one sirloin from the back. Push/roll the meat down over the ribs. Cut it free as soon as there is no more meat between the skin and ribs. Pull or cut off the skin and set aside.

4 Lay the first sirloin along the rectangle of escalopes. Do the same with the other sirloin. Lay the bacon in long strips around the sirloins.

5 Cut free the fillets (the tiny triangular strips of meat on the inner side of the ribs towards the haunch) and slot them into the meat strips wherever they will fit.

6 Roughly crush the garlic and all the herbs and rub them into the leg meat and sirloins of the hare. Pour over half of the olive oil and the lemon juice and complete the filling with half of the tritto.

7 Roll up the outer leg meat so the whole hare now resembles a fat and untidy sausage. Secure it with loops of string.

8 In as tight fitting a casserole dish as you can find, brown the tritto in the remaining oil. Add the hare and brown it evenly. Roughly chop the tomatoes and add them and the wine to the dish.

9 Cover and bake in the oven for about 1½ hours, or until very tender.

10 Season the saucepan juices, remove the string and carve the roulade. Serve with the juices spooned over it.

Roast Rabbit with Lamb

Serves 8–10

1 large lamb shoulder – weighing about 2 kg
    (4½ lb), cut into 8 large bones – in chunks
1 large rabbit, jointed into 8 (4 legs with the
    saddle cut into 4 pieces)
1 large onion, sliced
4 cloves garlic, roughly crushed
4 good sprigs rosemary
12 fresh sage leaves
300 ml (10 fl oz) dry white wine
4 tbsp dry Marsala
salt and freshly ground black pepper

Cook's Tip

This reasonably cunning combination links two meats with very different, but highly complementary, basic qualities. The result is extremely interesting. You could just squeeze by with half a shoulder and half a rabbit if you want to cook for a smaller number but, really, bulk is best: the juices flow faster and stronger.

1   Preheat the oven to 180°C/350°F/Gas Mark 4. Heat a roasting tin until it is very hot. Add no oil. Drop in the lamb shoulder. Seal the lamb pieces by sautéeing very fiercely, then lower the heat until a little of the lamb fat begins to run. Remove the lamb and set aside.

2   Add the jointed rabbit. Seal the rabbit gently for 2–3 minutes. Remove from the baking tray and set aside.

3   Scorch the onion in what should be a very lightly greased roasting tin. Add the garlic, rosemary, sage and the wines. Bring everything to a boil.

4   Replace the meat, making sure the pieces alternate with each other: the fat of the lamb must moisten the rabbit during cooking and the flavor of the rabbit must permeate the lamb. Season at this point.

5   Cover and bake in the oven for about 1½ hours until tender.

Pigeon Breasts with Pine Nuts and Lemon

Serves 4

6 young pigeons
50 g (2 oz) Tritto (see page 138)
50 g (2 oz) pine nuts
4 tbsp olive oil
juice and peel of 1 lemon
150 ml (1pt) Marsala

1 Remove the breasts from the pigeons. Keeping the blade very close to the high-ridged breastbone, a swift stroke of the knife from back to front will have the breast hanging on by the skin only. Cut through the skin. Brown the tritto in a very large saucepan. Roughly chop the carcasses. As the tritto browns, add them, cover with water and bring to a boil. Let simmer.

2 In a frying pan containing no oil, toast the pine nuts until they begin to brown. Remove them from the heat immediately – they will continue to cook a little.

3 Heat the olive oil in a heavy saucepan and add each pigeon breast. Cook for no more than 10 seconds on each side. The breasts will puff up. Remove the skin, then slice each breast through across the horizontal – flat – plane. Seal the raw sides of each breast for 2–3 seconds in the hot oil.

4 Pour away most of the oil and return the saucepan to high heat. Add the lemon juice, peel and the Marsala and reduce until you have a thick syrup, about 5 minutes. Stir in 50 ml (2 fl oz) of the pigeon broth made from the carcasses and reduce again.

5 Toss the breasts into the sauce and reheat for 30 seconds. Remove the breasts from the saucepan, pour the sauce over them and sprinkle the browned pine nuts on top.

Duck with Anchovies

Serves 4
10 flat anchovy fillets
8 cloves garlic, chopped
1 onion, sliced
1 carrot, sliced
1 celery stick, sliced
few slices fresh ginger, sliced
75 g (3 oz) pitted green olives
vegetable oil
1¾ kg (4 lb) duck, cut into pieces
salt
chicken stock

1   Put the anchovies, garlic, vegetables, ginger and olives into a large saucepan. Coat with a few tbsp oil and fry for 5 minutes.

2   Add the duck pieces to the saucepan with a pinch of salt if desired (the anchovies are salty so minimal salt is needed) and brown over a high heat.

3   Cover and cook over a medium heat for 45 minutes, adding a little chicken stock where necessary to prevent the duck from drying out.

MEAT

Meat – beef and veal, pork and lamb – plays just as important a part in Italian cooking as it does in other cuisines. Roast and grilled meat is very popular – veal is a firm favorite – but there are also recipes for delicious stews and other slow cooked dishes, such as Osso Buco or Pork Pot-Roast in Milk. Offal is also an often-used ingredient, and the basis for some truly classic Italian meat dishes.

Veal Piccata

Serves 4
450 g (1 lb) veal escalopes
2 tbsp butter
2 tbsp olive oil
50 g (2 oz) all-purpose flour
juice of 2 lemons
2 tbsp finely chopped fresh parsley
salt and freshly ground black pepper
handful of capers

1 Cut the veal into four equal slices and batten into escalopes.
2 Melt the butter with the oil over a high heat. Dip each escalope into the flour, shake off the excess and fry rapidly – about 1 minute each side. Set the escalopes aside in a warm place.
3 Over a high heat, add the lemon juice to the pan juices with the parsley. Return the escalopes to the pan to warm them through – seconds only, for they are already cooked.
4 Serve immediately, seasoned to taste.

Tuscan Veal with Prosciutto

Serves 4
1 kg (2 lb) veal rump roast
salt and freshly ground black pepper
all-purpose flour
3 tbsp butter
vegetable oil
1 onion, chopped
100 g (4 oz) prosciutto, cut into strips
250 ml (8 fl oz) dry red wine
2 medium potatoes, boiled, peeled, cut into chunks
1 clove garlic, crushed
zest of 1 lemon
ground nutmeg

1 Season the meat with salt and pepper and flour lightly. Melt the butter in a heavy-based saucepan, add a little oil and brown the meat. Stir in the onion and prosciutto, pour in the wine and cook over high heat until the liquid has almost evaporated. Cover the meat with water and continue to cook, turning occasionally. Just before the veal is done, add the potatoes and stir in garlic, lemon zest and nutmeg; let flavors mingle. Put the meat on a serving dish, pour over the cooking juices, surround with potatoes and serve immediately.

Osso Buco

Serves 4

2 tbsp olive oil
225 g (8 oz) Tritto (see page 138)
4 veal shin cutlets (each weighing about
    175 g (6 oz)
300 ml (10 fl oz) dry white wine
350 g (12 oz) fresh or canned plum tomatoes,
    roughly chopped
25 g (1 oz) green olives, pitted and halved
2 fresh bay leaves
1 tbsp finely chopped fresh parsley
7½ g (¼ oz) thyme (fresh or dried)
salt and freshly ground black pepper
2 tbsp finely chopped fresh basil

1 Preheat the oven to 180°C/350°F/Gas Mark 4.
  Over medium heat, toss the oil and tritto together
  until the tritto softens – about 3 minutes.
2 Increase the heat and add the veal shin cutlets.
  Seal them well on both sides. Now lift out the tritto
  vegetables and meat with a slotted spoon. Pour
  off most of the oil.
3 Replace the ingredients and, over high heat, add
  the wine, tomatoes, olives, bay leaves, chopped
  parsley and thyme.
4 Bring everything to a rolling boil, then cover well.
  Bake in the oven for about 1¼ hours until tender.
5 When the veal is cooked, lift it out and set it in a
  warm place. Boil the sauce vigorously to reduce
  its volume by about one-third. Season with the salt
  and pepper, throw in the fresh basil, pour over the
  meat and serve.

Genoese Meatballs

Serves 4

400 g (14 oz) cooked veal, ground
3 tbsp fresh breadcrumbs, soaked in stock or
    milk and squeezed dry
1 clove garlic, crushed
1 bunch parsley, chopped
few fresh marjoram leaves
2 tbsp dried mushrooms, soaked, drained
    and chopped
2 tbsp grated Parmesan cheese
salt and freshly ground black pepper
ground nutmeg
1 egg, beaten
all-purpose flour
vegetable oil
2tbsp butter

1 In a bowl, mix the veal, breadcrumbs, garlic,
  parsley, marjoram, mushrooms and cheese.
  Season with salt, pepper and nutmeg. Blend in
  the egg, mixing well.
2 Form the mixture into balls, flatten slightly and
  dip in flour.
3 Brown quickly in plenty of oil and butter, then
  reduce the heat and continue to fry until cooked
  through. Serve hot.

Veal Kidneys with Mushrooms

Serves 4
1 tbsp chopped onion
1 clove garlic, crushed
vegetable oil
4 fresh mushrooms, sliced
salt and freshly ground black pepper
2 x 225 g (8 oz) veal kidneys, without fat or skin
50 g (2 oz) butter
chopped parsley
2 slices bread

1 Fry the onion and garlic in oil, add the mushrooms, season with salt and pepper and cook through over medium heat.
2 In another frying pan, sauté the kidneys in half of the butter and a few tbsp oil until done. Season, add the mushroom mixture and cook briefly. Put on a serving dish, sprinkle with parsley and garnish with bread cut into triangles and fried in the remaining butter and a little oil.

Veal Cutlets with Pecorino

Serves 4
4 veal cutlets
white wine vinegar
salt and freshly ground black pepper
3 cloves garlic, crushed
2 eggs, beaten
5 tbsp grated Pecorino cheese
breadcrumbs
vegetable oil

1 Flatten the cutlets slightly. Put on a plate, sprinkle on a little vinegar and marinate for an hour or so. Drain, pat dry and season with salt and pepper.
2 Mix the garlic into the beaten eggs; mix the pecorino with the breadcrumbs. Dip the cutlets first into the egg, then into the breadcrumb mixture, pressing the coating on firmly. Fry in hot oil until browned and crisp on both sides. Drain on paper towels and serve.

Veal Scallopini with Parma Ham

Serves 4

8 veal cutlets
salt and freshly ground black pepper
8 slices of prosciutto
8 fresh sage leaves
all-purpose flour
5 tbsp butter
120 ml (4 fl oz) dry white wine

1   Flatten the veal cutlets and sprinkle with salt and pepper. Cover each cutlet with a slice of prosciutto and a sage leaf, then fold each one in half and secure with a toothpick. Flour lightly.

2   Heat 4 tbsp butter in a frying pan and fry the veal over medium-high heat until brown all over and cooked through. Remove with a slotted spoon and arrange on a serving dish.

3   Add the wine to the cooking juices and reduce almost completely. Add the remaining butter and stir until melted; pour the hot sauce over the veal. Serve immediately.

Stuffed Shoulder of Veal

Serves 4

1 small onion, sliced
150 g (5 oz) sliced sausage
5 tbsp/65 g (2^{1}/$_{2}$ oz) butter
150 g (5 oz) rice
salt and freshly ground black pepper
1 l (2 pt) boiling chicken stock
1 bunch parsley, chopped
250 ml (8 fl oz) dry white wine
25 g (1 oz) grated Parmesan cheese
750 g (1^{3}/$_{4}$ lb) shoulder of veal in one piece
rosemary sprig
vegetable oil

1   Preheat the oven to 190°C/375°F/Gas Mark 5. Fry the onion and sausage in half of the butter. Add the rice and season with salt and pepper; then cook, adding the boiling stock gradually and stirring frequently. When the rice is almost tender, add the parsley and half of the wine and leave the risotto on the heat until the wine is completely absorbed. Sprinkle on grated Parmesan cheese.

2   Flatten out the veal, season and spread with risotto. Roll up the meat, insert the rosemary, secure with toothpicks and put in a saucepan with the remaining butter and a few tbsp oil. Roast until brown, turning the meat frequently.

3   After 30 minutes, pour over the remaining wine and roast for 1 more hour. Remove from the oven, slice the meat and serve immediately.

Pot Roast Beef with Cinnamon

Serves 4

3 onions, thickly sliced
6 tbsp butter
2 tbsp vegetable oil
750 g (1³/₄ lb) boneless beef chuck roast
salt and freshly ground black pepper
pinch of ground cinnamon
juice of 1 lemon
120 ml (4 fl oz) dry white wine
1 bay leaf

1 Put the onions into a saucepan with the butter and oil. Cook over low heat for 5 minutes. Add the meat; sprinkle with salt, pepper and cinnamon. Pour in the lemon juice and wine, add the bay leaf, cover and cook over low heat for 2½ hours, turning the meat occasionally.

2 When the meat is tender, remove from the saucepan, slice and arrange on a serving dish. Pour over the hot sauce from the pan and serve immediately.

Beef in Red Wine

Serves 4

6 tbsp butter
750 g (1³/₄ lb) stewing beef
450 g (1 lb) onions, sliced
salt and freshly ground black pepper
250 ml (8 fl oz) condensed beef stock
a bottle of robust red wine

1 Preheat the oven to 190°C/375°F/Gas Mark 5. Heat the margarine or butter in a saucepan and brown the meat in it. Remove with a slotted spoon and transfer to a plate. Then add the onions and cook until very soft but not browned. (Add a little water if necessary).

2 When the onions are very soft, arrange in a casserole dish and put the meat on top. Season with salt and pepper and add the stock. Then add just enough wine to cover. Bake until the sauce is reduced and the meat is tender (about 1 hour) and serve hot with sautéed potatoes and mixed Italian vegetables.

Steak with Anchovies

Serves 4
8 flat anchovy fillets
100 g (4 oz) butter
freshly ground black pepper
4 x 100 g (4 oz) beef steaks
salt
75 g (3 oz) pitted green olives

1 Press four anchovy fillets through a strainer and put in a bowl. Roll up the remaining four anchovies and set aside. Add half of the butter and a pinch of pepper to the strained anchovies and mix to a smooth paste with a wooden spoon. Shape the mixture into a cylinder and wrap in foil. Place in the fridge for 1 hour.

2 Melt 1 tbsp/15 g (½ oz) butter in a saucepan and add the steaks. Cook over high heat for 2 minutes on each side. Drain, put in a dish, season with salt and pepper and keep warm.

3 Add the remaining butter to the cooking juices, stir in the olives and cook gently for 10 minutes, stirring occasionally. Take the anchovy butter from the fridge and cut into slices. Put a slice on each steak and top with a rolled anchovy. Garnish with olives, pour over the hot sauce and serve.

Beef Tenderloin with Capers

Serves 4
8 x 100 g (4 oz) slices beef tenderloin
salt and freshly ground black pepper
all-purpose flour
5 tbsp butter
vegetable oil
50 g (2 oz) capers
1 tbsp chopped parsley
2–3 tbsp vinegar
ground nutmeg

1 Pound the beef slices lightly so all are the same shape. Sprinkle with salt and pepper; dust lightly with flour. Heat the butter with a little oil in a saucepan. Brown the meat; then add the capers, parsley and 2 tbsp cold water and cook, stirring frequently.

2 In a separate saucepan, heat the vinegar with nutmeg over high heat, pour over the meat and stir again. Serve the meat on a platter, covered with sauce.

Fillet of Beef with Orange

Serves 4
1 tbsp olive oil
4 fillet mignon, each weighing about 175 g (6 oz)
4 tbsp Marsala
4 tbsp red wine
2 Seville oranges
salt and freshly ground black pepper

1 Heat the oil in a heavy frying pan. Brown the steaks for one minute on each side. Lift from the frying pan and set them aside in a warm place (an oven at 150°C/275°F/Gas Mark 1).
2 Over very high heat, add the Marsala and red wine to deglaze the pan. Lower the heat, zest the oranges and add both juice and zest to the pan.
3 For meat cooked medium, return the steaks to the pan and reheat them as the juices reduce. For rare, cook the wine and juice to a light syrup consistency before you return the meat.
4 To serve, pour the juices over each steak. Sprinkle with salt and a generous amount of coarsely ground black pepper before eating.

Beef Kebabs with Mushrooms and Prunes

Serves 4
16 prunes
about 500 g (1¼ lb) lean, boneless beef,
   cut into 12 equal cubes
12 mushroom caps
8 bay leaves
salt and pepper
1 tsp ground thyme
olive oil

1 Soak the prunes in lukewarm water for 1 hour, then drain and pit. Preheat the oven to 220°C/425°F/ Gas Mark 7.
2 Thread the prunes, beef cubes and mushrooms alternately onto four metal skewers. Put a bay leaf at each end. Season the kebabs with salt, pepper and thyme and sprinkle with olive oil.
3 Put in an oiled baking dish and bake for 10 minutes, turning and basting with cooking juices. Transfer to a serving dish and serve very hot.

Steak with Parma Ham and Eggs

Serves 4
6 tbsp butter
100 g (4 oz) beef steaks
salt and freshly ground black pepper
4 slices prosciutto
4 eggs

1 Melt half of the butter in a saucepan and add the steaks. Cook over high heat for 2 minutes on each side. Drain, season with salt and pepper and keep hot.
2 Melt the remaining butter into the saucepan. Add the prosciutto and cook gently for 2 minutes. Break an egg onto each slice of prosciutto and cook until the whites have set. Season the eggs and lift out the prosciutto with a spatula. Top the steaks with prosciutto and eggs and pour over the juices from the pan. Serve immediately.

Steak with Gorgonzola Butter

Serves 4
6 tbsp butter
25 g (1 oz) mild Gorgonzola cheese, crumbled
1 tbsp chopped parsley
lemon juice
4 x 100 g (4 oz) beef steaks
salt and freshly ground black pepper

1. Put 4 tbsp butter, the Gorgonzola, parsley and a few drops of lemon juice into a bowl and beat with a wooden spoon until the mixture is smooth and creamy. Roll the mixture into a cylinder and wrap in foil. Refrigerate for 1 hour.

2. Melt the remaining butter in a saucepan, add the steaks and cook over high heat for 2 minutes on each side. Drain, season with salt and pepper and put on a serving dish.

3. Cut the Gorgonzola butter into 12 slices and put three slices on each steak. Serve piping hot.

Croquettes with Mozzarella and Lemon

Serves 4

450 g (1 lb) lean ground beef
5 large slices stale bread, crusts trimmed,
    soaked in water and squeezed dry
3 tbsp chopped parsley
6 tbsp grated Parmesan cheese
salt and pepper
2 eggs, beaten
175 g (6 oz) diced mozzarella cheese
all-purpose flour
vegetable oil
lemon wedges

1 Combine the beef, bread, parsley and Parmesan in a bowl. Season with salt and pepper, then blend in the eggs. Form into four croquettes and press the mozzarella into the centres; re-shape the croquettes.

2 Roll in flour and fry in plenty of hot oil. Serve with lemon wedges.

Croquettes with Mozzarella and Tomato

Serves 4

450 g (1 lb) lean ground beef
5 large slices stale bread, crusts trimmed,
    soaked in water and squeezed dry
4 tbsp chopped parsley
50 g (2 oz) grated Parmesan cheese
salt and pepper
2 eggs, beaten
175 g (6 oz) diced mozzarella cheese
all-purpose flour
vegetable oil
2 tbsp chopped onion
450 g (1 lb) tomatoes, peeled, de-seeded and
    pressed through a strainer
coarsely chopped fresh basil

1 Combine the beef, bread, parsley and Parmesan in a bowl. Season with salt and pepper, then blend in the eggs. Form the mixture into four oblong croquettes and press the mozzarella into them; re-shape the croquettes. Roll in the flour and fry in plenty of hot oil.

2 Meanwhile, fry the onion in a saucepan with a few tbsp oil, add the tomatoes, season and cook over medium heat for about 20 minutes. Arrange the croquettes in the simmering sauce and leave to absorb the flavors, scooping the sauce on top. Garnish with basil.

Pot-Roasted Lamb with Juniper

Serves 4

1 large shoulder of lamb, weighing about
 1 kg (2 lb)
100g (4 oz) Tritto (see page 138)
300 ml (10 fl oz) dry white wine
2 good sprigs fresh rosemary
1 tbsp juniper berries
salt and pepper to taste

1 Preheat the oven to 180°C/350°F/Gas Mark 4.
   Heat, if available, a flameproof and ovenproof
   casserole dish, without oil.
2 When the casserole dish is really hot, drop in the
   lamb shoulder. Sear it for a minute on each side.
   Remove from the heat.
3 Add the tritto, white wine, rosemary and juniper
   berries to the casserole dish. Cover well and put
   in the oven for approximately 2½ hours (oven
   cookers vary so you may need to cook for longer).
   After 1 hour, check the liquid and top it up to its
   original volume with water, if necessary.
4 Thirty minutes before serving, remove the lid.
   Season the juices with salt and pepper, and carve
   to serve.

Pork Pot-Roast in Milk

Serves 6
4 tbsp butter
1 kg (2 lb) joint of de-boned pork (loin or leg)
600 ml (1 pt) milk
salt and freshly ground black pepper
8 fresh sage leaves
2 bay leaves

1. Preheat the oven to 180°C/350°F/Gas Mark 4. Melt the butter over medium heat in the dish you are going to use for the pork – a casserole dish with a lid if you have one.
2. When the butter begins to foam, add the joint and brown on all sides. Now slowly pour in the milk. The stream should be slow enough to boil as soon as it hits the pot. Season with the salt and pepper and add the sage and bay leaves.
3. Loosely cover the pot – with its own lid or with foil, if you're using a roasting tin – and place it in the oven.
4. Turn the joint completely after 1 hour. Top up the milk at that point if the level is below half. Roast for another hour.
5. When the joint is cooked, let it stand for 10 minutes or so before carving. This gives you time to make the sauce.
6. If the milk is still creamy and pale, boil it down until it begins to caramelize. If not, immediately add 120 ml (4 fl oz) or so of water to the saucepan and de-glaze. (Don't be tempted to use wine or stock here. What you are after is the pure flavor of the pan juices, milk and herbs.)
7. Carve the meat, spoon the sauce over it and serve immediately.

Lamb and Artichoke Casserole

Serves 4

700 g (1½ lb) lean boneless lamb (leg or shoulder), cubed
5 tbsp butter
vegetable oil
salt and freshly ground black pepper
chicken stock
8 tinned artichoke hearts
120 ml (4 fl oz) dry white wine
chopped parsley

1 Brown the meat in 5 tbsp butter and a little oil, season with salt and pepper and cook over low heat until tender, adding stock as necessary. Cut the artichoke hearts into strips and cook in the remaining butter with a pinch of salt.
2 Put the lamb onto a dish, add wine to the cooking juices and reduce. Pour onto the lamb, garnish with artichokes, sprinkle with parsley and serve.

Lamb Cutlets in Mushroom Sauce

Serves 4

For the sauce
½ small onion, chopped
50 g (2 oz) butter
25 g (1 oz) fresh mushrooms, sliced
salt and pepper
ground nutmeg
dry white wine
350 ml (12 fl oz) condensed chicken stock
1 tbsp all-purpose flour

2 egg yolks
250 ml (8 fl oz) half and half
squeeze of lemon juice

For the lamb
8 boneless lamb loin chops
100 g (4 oz) butter
salt
2 eggs, beaten
breadcrumbs
parsley

1 First make the sauce. Fry the onion in 2 tbsp butter, add the mushrooms, season with salt, pepper and nutmeg, moisten with a little white wine and cook, adding 175 ml (6 fl oz) stock gradually.
2 Melt the remaining butter in a saucepan, mix in the flour and gradually blend in 120 ml/(4 fl oz) stock. Cook, stirring, until slightly thickened. Beat together the egg yolks and remaining stock; blend the yolk mixture into the mushroom mixture, then stir all into the hot sauce.
3 Blend in the cream and lemon juice. Adjust the seasoning and stir over low heat until the sauce has thickened. (Do not allow the sauce to boil.)
4 Then cook the cutlets, browning them in 50 g (2 oz) butter. Season with salt, remove from the pan and leave to cool. Cover the cutlets completely with egg and breadcrumbs. Heat the remaining butter in the saucepan and brown the breaded cutlets. Drain, garnish with parsley and serve with the hot mushroom sauce.

Baked Country Kebabs with Rice

Serves 4

450 g (1 lb) lean, boneless pork (leg or shoulder)
3 zucchini
75 g (3 oz) fresh mushrooms
2 firm tomatoes
3 peppers, de-seeded, cut into slices
salt and freshly ground black pepper
25 g (1 oz) all-purpose flour
vegetable oil
1 onion, chopped
250 ml (8 fl oz) dry white wine
250 g (9 oz) Arborio rice

1 Cut the pork into chunks. Cut the zucchini, mushrooms and tomatoes into slices. Thread the meat, zucchini, mushrooms, tomatoes and peppers alternately onto four wooden skewers. Sprinkle with salt and pepper; flour lightly.

2 Heat some oil in an ovenproof casserole dish and lightly brown the kebabs. Add the onion and pour in half of the wine. Cover and cook for 10 minutes, without reducing the sauce.

3 Preheat the oven to 200°C/400°F/Gas Mark 6. Spoon the rice around the meat; add the remaining wine and enough water to cover. Bring to a boil. Cover and bake for 20 minutes. Let stand for 5 minutes before serving.

Sweet and Sour Lamb

Serves 4

1 kg (2 lb) lamb shoulder
2 cloves garlic
fresh rosemary leaves
½ onion, sliced
vegetable oil
salt and freshly ground black pepper
450 g (1 lb) tomatoes, peeled, de-seeded and pressed through a strainer
120 ml (4 fl oz) red wine vinegar
4 tsp sugar

1 Wash the lamb, pat dry and stick with slivers of garlic and rosemary leaves. Fry the onion in a heavy-based saucepan with a few spoonfuls of oil; then brown the meat, season with salt and pepper and add the tomatoes. Cover and cook for 45 minutes.

2 Add the vinegar and let some evaporate. Then add the sugar and simmer for 45 minutes longer, adding a few spoonfuls of water or stock as necessary. Serve the meat sliced and covered with hot sauce.

Calves' Liver with Onion

Serves 4

2 tbsp olive oil
6 medium onions, very finely sliced
2 leaves fresh sage
1 kg (2 lb) calves' liver
4 tbsp dry white wine
salt and freshly ground black pepper

1 Heat the oil and add the onions. Cook until they are soft and medium brown in color. Roughly tear up the sage leaves and mix them into the onions when they are cooked.

2 Now remove the onions from the saucepan with a slotted spoon and reserve.

3 Slice the liver into thin strips and increase the heat to high. Add the liver when the saucepan is very hot. As soon as each piece is sealed, take out the liver (see Chef's tip) and mix it with the onions.

4 Return the saucepan to high heat and deglaze it with the white wine. When all has practically evaporated, return the onions and liver to the pan, reheat for a few seconds, season and serve immediately with mashed potatoes.

Roast Leg of Pork

Serves 4

1½ kg (3 lb) leg of pork
120 ml (4 fl oz) olive oil
salt and freshly ground black pepper
175 ml (6 fl oz) hot chicken stock
1 tbsp whole cloves
100 g (4 oz) sugar
150 ml (5 fl oz) dry white wine
4 tbsp vinegar
cornstarch

1 Soak the pork in cold water for 2 hours, then drain and pat dry. Preheat the oven to 160°C/325°F/Gas Mark 3. Pour the oil into a large casserole. Season the meat with salt and pepper and add to the casserole. Roast for 3 hours, basting occasionally with a little hot stock.

2 Place the meat on a plate, and skim fat from the pan. Pour the juices out of the roasting pan and reserve. With a sharp knife, cut crosses into the rind of the pork leg; put a clove into each cross and sprinkle the surface with sugar. Put the leg back into the roasting pan and return to the oven at 190°C/375°F/Gas Mark 5 until the sugar caramelizes.

3 Mix the wine with the vinegar and reserved drippings and pour this mixture over the meat. Cook for 1 more hour. Transfer the pork to a serving dish. Skim the fat from the cooking juices, strain the remaining liquid and bring to a boil. Thicken the gravy with cornstarch. Pour it into a gravy boat and serve with the leg of pork.

Pork Chops with Olives

Serves 4

20 cloves garlic
4 pork chops
vegetable oil
vinegar
rosemary sprig
few fresh sage leaves
salt and feshly ground black pepper
100 g (4 oz) large green olives
1 tbsp butter
4 tbsp Marsala or white wine
1 tbsp chopped parsley

1. Peel 18 cloves of garlic; cook for 3 minutes in boiling water, then drain. Flatten the chops and sprinkle with the remaining garlic, cut into slivers. Prepare a marinade with the oil, a little vinegar, rosemary, sage, salt and pepper. Marinate the chops for 2 hours, turning occasionally. Drain and pat dry.

2. Boil the olives in water to cover for 10 minutes, remove from heat and keep hot in the cooking liquid.

3. Heat the butter in a saucepan with 1 tbsp oil and add the chops; brown for 3 minutes on each side. Reduce the heat, add the drained garlic and continue to cook for 12 minutes longer or until the chops are cooked through, turning occasionally.

4. Put the chops on a plate and pile the garlic and drained olives in the center. Pour the Marsala or wine into the pan juices and reduce slightly; simmer for 5 minutes, then pour the sauce onto the chops. Sprinkle with chopped parsley and serve.

Ham Slices with Anchovy Sauce

Serves 4

8 x 75 g (3 oz) slices ham
freshly ground black pepper
1 tsp all-purpose flour
2 eggs, beaten
few tbsp fresh breadcrumbs
7 tbsp butter
1 small onion, chopped
5 flat anchovy fillets, rinsed and well mashed
1 tbsp capers, chopped
1 tbsp chopped parsley
vinegar
chicken stock

1 Flatten the ham slices with a mallet and season with pepper; then dip in flour, egg and breadcrumbs.

2 Melt 2 tbsp butter in a saucepan, add the onion and cook over low heat until soft. Add the anchovies, capers, parsley, flour and a little pepper. Stir over high heat for a few minutes; stir in 2–3 tbsp vinegar and let evaporate. Add enough stock to give a slightly thickened sauce. Dice 1 tbsp butter and stir into the sauce a piece at a time, making sure that each piece is fully incorporated before adding the next. Keep warm.

3 In a separate saucepan, melt the remaining butter; add the breaded ham slices and brown on both sides, then reduce the heat and cook for 10–12 minutes, turning occasionally. Arrange on a serving dish, pour over the sauce and serve with buttered spinach.

Sweetbreads with Rosemary and Peas

Serves 4–6

1 carrot, roughly chopped
1 stick celery, roughly chopped
2 small onions
½ lemon
675 g (1½ lb) sweetbreads
5 tbsp olive oil
300 ml (10 fl oz) dry white wine
350 g (12 oz) shelled peas, fresh or frozen
1 good sprig fresh rosemary
1 chili
salt and freshly ground black pepper

1 Bring 2 l (4 pt) water to a boil and add the roughly chopped carrot and celery, 1 onion and the ½ lemon. Poach the sweetbreads in the stock for 5 minutes.

2 Remove the sweetbreads. You will be able to see the membrane around them. Carefully remove as much of this as you can and then set aside.

3 Heat the olive oil over medium heat. Finely slice the other onion and sauté it in the oil. Add the sweetbreads, sliced into 2½ cm (1 in) chunks, and brown them over medium heat with the onions for about 3–4 minutes. Add the white wine, peas – if using fresh ones – the rosemary and the whole chili. Cover the saucepan and poach the sweetbreads for 15–20 minutes. Remove the sweetbreads and set them aside.

4 Over very high heat, reduce the cooking liquid until there is just enough left to glaze the sweetbreads. Return them to the saucepan, with the frozen peas, if using. Season and serve as soon as everything is hot.

Calves' Brains with Tomato Dressing

Serves 6

2 calves' brains
juice of 1 lemon
1 medium carrot
½ medium fennel bulb
1 small onion
4 tbsp vinegar
175 ml (6 fl oz) olive oil
225 g (8 oz) fresh plum
    tomatoes

25 g (1 oz) fresh basil
salt and freshly
    ground black
    pepper
175 g (6 oz) fine fresh
    breadcrumbs
1½ tbsp freshly grated
    Parmesan cheese
2 eggs

1. Soak the calves' brains in cold water and lemon juice.

2. Chop the carrot, fennel and onion roughly bring 1 l (2 pt) water to a boil and add the vegetables and the vinegar.

3. Drain the brains, peel off any obvious membrane and drop them into the boiling water. Poach at a low simmer for 15 minutes.

4. As the brains are cooking, divide the oil between two bowls. Skin the tomatoes and chop them roughly and finely chop the basil. Mix the tomatoes, basil, salt and pepper in one bowl of oil, and transfer to a serving dish.

5. Drain the brains, pat them dry and set them aside in the fridge or another cool place.

6. Mix the breadcrumbs and the cheese in a shallow dish. Break the eggs and beat them in a shallow bowl.

7. Slice the brains widthways into 1 cm (½ in) rounds, dip each in the egg, shake off any excess, then press each side firmly into the breadcrumbs.

8. Fry them in the remaining olive oil over medium heat until the breadcrumbs form a crisp crust. Serve with the tomato and basil sauce underneath.

DESSERTS

Cheese and fresh fruit are the traditional Italian puddings, but on Sundays and special occasions meals can be rounded off with elaborate concoctions of cream, chocolate and meringue on a cake base soaked in liqueur. In addition to some of the sumptuous Italian desserts that can be made at home, this section also includes a selection of dessert cookies. In Italy, these may be eaten at any time of the day – nibbled with coffee or an early morning glass of wine, or enjoyed after a heavy meal with a warming and syrupy liqueur.

Italian Fruit Salad

Serves 6
300 ml (10 fl oz) fresh orange juice
zest and juice of 1 lemon
2 apples
2 firm pears
2 firm bananas
675 g (1½ lb) assorted fruit: peaches, apricots,
   melon, grapes, cherries etc
4 tbsp granulated sugar
4 tbsp grappa or Grand Marnier

1 Mix the orange juice, lemon juice and zest.
2 Peel all the fruit except the grapes and cherries. De-seed everything. As each fruit is peeled, chop it into grape size and add it to the fruit juice mixture immediately to stop it discoloring in the air.
3 Sprinkle the sugar over, pour on the liqueur and chill for at least 4 hours if you can. Stir the mixture – carefully – 2 or 3 times during the chilling process.

Fragolini Fritti (Fried Strawberries)

Serves 6
50 g (2 oz) all-purpose flour
2 tbsp butter, melted
1 egg
milk
brandy
450 g (1 lb) strawberries
5 tbsp sugar
4 tbsp cherry liqueur
vegetable oil for deep-frying
25 g (1 oz) icing sugar

1 Sift the flour into a bowl and mix in the butter. Add the egg and enough milk and brandy to make a smooth batter. Leave to stand for 1 hour.
2 Trim and wash the strawberries, then spread out on a plate. Sprinkle with the sugar and maraschino and leave stand for about 30 minutes. Ten minutes before serving, beat the egg white until stiff and fold into the batter.
3 Dip the strawberries into the batter one by one, coating well, and deep fry in plenty of oil until golden brown and crisp. Drain on paper towels. Put on a dish, sprinkle with icing sugar and serve.

Timbale of Pears in Red Wine

Serves 4
For the filling
450 g (1 lb) pears,
   peeled and cored
red wine
sugar
1 whole clove
pinch of ground
   cinnamon

For the pastry
100 g (4 oz) all-purpose
   flour
150 g (5 oz) superfine
   sugar
90 g (2½ oz) yellow
   polenta
150 g (5 oz) butter
pinch salt
3 egg yolks

1 For the filling, cut the pears into chunks and cook until tender in red wine with a little sugar and the spices. Remove the clove; set the pears aside.
2 For the pastry, combine the flour, sugar, polenta, butter (except for about 1 tbsp), salt and egg yolks, adding a little water, if necessary. Cover and chill for about 1 hour.
3 Preheat the oven to 190°C/375°F/Gas Mark 5. Roll out a little over half of the pastry and line a tart pan fill with the pears. Dot with the reserved butter. Roll out the remaining pastry; make a lattice top and place on the pears. Bake until golden brown.

Tiramisu

Serves 8
4 eggs
4 tbsp marsala
100 g (4 oz) powdered sugar
225 g (8 oz) mascarpone
300 ml (½ pt) strong coffee, sweetened with
    50 g (2 oz) white sugar
40 lady fingers – about 8 x 2 cm
    (3 x 1 in) each
4 tbsp cocoa

1 Separate the eggs and the yolks. Set aside two whites in another bowl. Combine the yolks, the wine and the sugar and beat them together.
2 Bring a saucepan of water to just below boiling, then turn down to simmer. Place the bowl with the egg yolks over the water and whisk the yolk mixture until it begins to swell and thicken. (Use a double-boiler or saucepan, if you have one.) Set the yolk mixture aside.
3 Whisk the two remaining whites into stiff peaks and fold them into the yolk mixture, then set aside.
4 Blend the cheese in a processor or blender and fold the yolk and white mixture into it. Check the sweetness at this stage and adjust it to taste.
5 Dip each lady finger in the coffee, allowing it to soak up the liquid. Arrange the sponge fingers on a dish, then spread with a thin coating of the egg/cheese mixture. Repeat the process until you have used all the mixture.
6 Sprinkle cocoa over the sides and top. Chill until completely cold and set.

Zabaglione

Serves 6
6 egg yolks
100 g (4 oz) powdered sugar
6 tbsp Marsala
raspberries to serve

1 Beat the egg yolks with the sugar and the wine.
2 Transfer the mixture into a bowl and place over a saucepan of simmering water. Beat the mixture with a balloon whisk or an electrical whisk. As air is incorporated into the eggs, it will swell. It will also stiffen as the heat of the water cooks it. Whisk until the mixture increases its volume by at least three times and stiffens until it is only just pourable.
3 Pour into glasses and serve with raspberries.

Cook's Tip

With a very good whisk, this dessert is stunningly simple. The caveat is the usual one with eggs and double boilers: don't let the water boil so that it overcooks the eggs. You can control the process quite finely by lifting the saucepan in and out of the hot water bath.

Here are some unorthodox variations:

1. Add the grated zest of an orange to the egg mixture before cooking.

2. Add a thumb-sized lump of crystallized ginger very finely sliced.

3. Use port instead of Marsala.

Zabaglione can also be a rather classy substitute for cream. With strawberries, for example.

Honeyed Neapolitan Doughnuts

Serves 4
150 g (5 oz) all-purpose flour
3 eggs, beaten
100 g (4 oz) sugar
1½ tbsp butter
grated orange and lemon zest
75 g (3 oz) candied citrus peel, diced
1 tbsp brandy
salt
milk
vegetable oil for deep frying
250 g (9 oz) honey
cake decorations

1   Mix the flour with beaten eggs, 1 tbsp/15 g (½ oz) sugar, butter, a little orange and lemon zest, 3 tbsp candied citrus peel, brandy and a pinch of salt (add a little milk, if necessary). Shape the dough into a ball, cover and leave to stand for 1 hour.
2   Make thin sticks of dough and deep fry in hot oil until golden brown. Drain on paper towels. Into a saucepan (copper, if possible) put the honey, the remaining sugar and a few tbsp water. Bring to a gentle boil and simmer until the syrup turns a yellow color.
3   Reduce the heat and add the pastries, stirring constantly so they are coated in honey. Remove with a slotted spoon, put onto a wet dish, and mold with your hands into ring doughnut shapes. Sprinkle cake decorations over them and decorate with the remaining candied peel cut into strips.

Sweet Baked Ravioli

Serves 6–8
For the pasta
425 g (15 oz) all-purpose flour
150 g (5 oz) butter
150 g (5 oz) sugar
4 eggs
25 g (1 oz) fresh yeast
120 ml (4 fl oz) lukewarm milk (35°C/95°F)

For the filling
250 g (9 oz) whole unpeeled chestnuts
50 g (2 oz) unsweetened cocoa powder
50 g (2 oz) sugar
50 g (2 oz) chopped almonds
50 g (2 oz) crushed Amaretti cookies
   (see page 168)
100 g (3 oz) orange marmalade

1   For the pasta, mix together the flour with the butter, sugar, three eggs and the yeast dissolved in lukewarm milk. Knead the dough for 20 minutes, cover and leave to rise in a warm place for an hour.
2   For the filling, boil the chestnuts, peel and press through a strainer or purée in a blender. Mix the chestnut purée with the cocoa, sugar, almonds, Amaretti and marmalade. Preheat the oven to 180°C/350°F/Gas Mark 4.
3   Roll out the pasta into a thin sheet and cut into circles 5 cm (2 in) in diameter. Place some filling on each; fold in half and press the edges to seal. Arrange on a greased baking sheet. Beat the remaining egg; brush over the ravioli. Bake for 20 minutes.

Ricotta Roll

Serves 2–4
For the pastry
225 g (8 oz) all-purpose flour
350 g (12 oz) butter or margarine
2 tbsp sugar
2 eggs
pinch salt
milk

For the filling
1 egg and 3 egg yolks
100 g (4 oz) superfine sugar
1 tbsp cornstarch
300 ml (10 fl oz) hot milk
1 tsp vanilla extract
75 g (3 oz) ricotta cheese
2 tbsp diced candied orange peel
1 egg, beaten (optional)
powdered sugar

1   Combine the ingredients for the pastry, adding
     enough milk to give the dough a soft, elastic
     consistency. Knead well, cover and chill for
     30 minutes.
2   For the filling, beat 1 egg and 3 egg yolks with the
     sugar, add the cornstarch and gradually mix in the
     milk and vanilla. Pour into a saucepan; place over
     low heat and bring to a boil, stirring constantly.
     Remove from the heat, leave to cool, and mix in the
     ricotta and orange peel.
3   Preheat the oven to 190°C/375°F/Gas Mark 5. Roll
     out the pastry on a floured board, then cut into
     rectangles. Put the filling on half of the rectangles
     and cover with the remaining rectangles, sealing
     the edges firmly. Brush with beaten egg, if desired.
     Arrange on a greased, floured baking sheet and
     bake until golden brown. Dust with icing sugar.

Orange and Grapefruit Salad

Serves 4
2 large oranges
3 large grapefruit
superfine sugar
liqueur

1   Peel the oranges and grapefruit and cut off all
     the white membranes. Cut the fruit clockways into
     slices, then cut the slices in half and arrange in a
     crystal bowl. Pour on the juice left on the chopping
     board and sprinkle with plenty of sugar and your
     choice of liqueur. Chill for an hour.

Amaretti

Makes 30 biscuits
210 g (7½ oz) blanched almonds
275 g (10 oz) superfine sugar
pinch of baking powder
4 egg whites
¼–½ tsp almond extract

1 Preheat the oven to 140°C/275°F/Gas Mark 1.
   Butter a baking sheet and flour it. Put the almonds
   and a little sugar in a mortar and pound into a
   powder. Pour the powder into a bowl with the
   remaining sugar and baking powder and stir.

2 Beat the egg whites until stiff; fold in the almond
   mixture, then the almond essence. Spoon into
   a pastry bag. Pipe the mixture onto the baking
   sheet, making small mounds. Bake until well dried
   (about 40 minutes) and let cool before serving.

Sweet Rice Croquettes San Giuseppe

Serves 4
50 g (2 oz) all-purpose flour
25 g (1 oz) fresh yeast
600 ml (1 pt) lukewarm milk (heated to 35°C/95°F)
90 g (3½ oz) rice
1 egg and 2 egg yolks
pinch salt
40 g (1½ oz) raisins, chopped
2 tbsp pine nuts
1 tbsp superfine sugar
grated zest of ½ lemon
vegetable oil
powdered sugar

1 Mix 3 tbsp flour with the crumbled yeast and mix with enough lukewarm milk to form a dough. Knead into a ball and cut a cross on top. Put the dough in a bowl and moisten the top with milk. Cover and leave to rise in a warm place for 20–30 minutes or until doubled in size.

2 Pour the remaining milk into a saucepan, bring to a boil, add the rice and cook, uncovered, over medium heat until tender. Pour the rice into a bowl and leave to cool, then add the remaining flour, egg, egg yolks, salt, yeast dough, raisins, pine nuts, sugar and lemon zest. Mix well, adding a few tbsp milk, if necessary.

3 Heat some oil in a frying pan, shape the rice mixture into balls and arrange in the frying pan (do not let the croquettes touch each other). Fry until golden brown, drain on paper towels, dust with powdered sugar and serve.

Sienese Spice Cake

Serves 10–12
1 tbsp coriander seeds
25 g (1 oz) unsweetened cocoa powder
2 tbsp ground cinnamon
1 whole nutmeg
3 cinnamon sticks
½ tsp whole cloves
6 whole black peppercorns
400 g (15 oz) blanched almonds
175 g (6 oz) honey
275 g (10 oz) superfine sugar
25 g (1 oz) finely chopped walnuts
100 g (4 oz) coarsely chopped candied orange peel
25 g (1 oz) coarsely chopped candied lemon peel
450 g (1 lb) mixed candied fruit, coarsely chopped
65 g (2½ oz) all-purpose flour
powdered sugar
pinch of ground cinnamon (optional)

1 First prepare two powders. Pound the coriander in a mortar and mix half of it with the cocoa and ground cinnamon. Grate the nutmeg; grind together with the cinnamon sticks, cloves, peppercorns and remaining coriander and set aside.

2 Preheat the oven to 180°C/350°F/Gas Mark 4. Toast the almonds until golden brown. Set aside. Put the honey and sugar in a copper saucepan over medium heat and stir constantly until the syrup has reached the soft ball stage. Remove from the heat; stir in the almonds, walnuts, orange peel, lemon peel, candied fruit, sifted flour and spice mixtures. Divide the mixture into two portions; spread each portion on a greased baking sheet in a 2½ cm (1 in) thick circle.

3 Place a pie plate on each circle and cut around the edges to make them even. Fasten a double thickness of foil around the edges of each circle to keep it in shape on the baking sheet.

4 Bake for 30 minutes. Let cool before removing from the baking sheet. Remove the foil with scissors and dust with powdered sugar mixed with cinnamon, if desired.

Sicilian Trifle Cake (Cassata)

Serves 8–10

450 g (1 lb) ricotta cheese
1 tbsp pistachio nuts
100 g (4 oz) dark chocolate pieces
20 g (4½ oz) mixed candied fruit
1 x 23 x 13 cm (9 x 5 in) loaf gingerbread
450 g (1 lb) superfine sugar
few drops vanilla extract
pinch ground cinnamon

For the topping

3 tbsp apricot jam
1 tbsp powdered sugar
3 tbsp superfine sugar
1 tbsp corn syrup
orange flower water
450 g (8 oz) mixed candied fruit

1 Line a 25 cm (10 in) springform pan with parchment paper. Place the ricotta in a bowl and beat until smooth. Blanch and peel the pistachios and pound in a mortar. Chop the chocolate and candied fruit. Cut the gingerbread into slices and line the saucepan with it, reserving a few slices.

2 Put the sugar and a few tbsp water in a saucepan; heat until the sugar has dissolved. To the ricotta, add the dissolved cooled sugar, vanilla, cinnamon, chocolate, candied fruit and pistachios. Put this into the saucepan, cover with the remaining gingerbread slices and then another layer of parchment paper. Push down and chill for a few hours.

3 Meanwhile, make the topping. Melt the apricot jam, add the powdered sugar and stir until dissolved. Remove the saucepan sides and invert the cake onto a plate; remove the parchment paper. Brush the cake with the jam mixture.

4 Over low heat, melt the superfine sugar and corn syrup, adding a few tbsp of orange flower water. Stir well, then pour onto the middle of the cake and spread all over it with a spatula.

5 Decorate the cake with candied fruit and let the topping set. Using two spatulas, lift the cake onto a serving dish. This classic topping for cassata is tinged with green from the pounded pistachio nuts and decorated with candied peel.

Cream Cake Deluxe

Serves 8–10

6 eggs
175 g (6 oz) superfine sugar
grated zest of 1 lemon
7 tbsp all-purpose flour
2 tbsp polenta

For the filling

100 g (4 oz) dark chocolate
25 g (1 oz) hazelnuts, toasted, skins rubbed off
25 g (1 oz) blanched almonds
6–8 tbsp liqueur
900 ml (2 pt) whipping cream
½ tsp vanilla extract
powdered chocolate
3 tbsp powdered sugar
glacé cherries (optional)

1 Prepare the cake the day before eating, as it will slice better. Grease and flour a deep 25 cm (10 in) round cake pan. Preheat the oven to 190°C/375°F/Gas Mark 5.

2 Using an electric whisk, beat the eggs and sugar together, add the lemon peel and sift in the flour. Fold in the semolina. Pour into the cake tin and bake for 40 minutes. Cool on a rack.

3 Melt the chocolate over low heat. Pour some of the chocolate into a icing bag with a fine tip. Pipe tiny circles of chocolate onto a sheet of parchment paper and leave to set. Meanwhile, pour the remaining chocolate onto another sheet of parchment paper, spread into a wide, thin sheet and leave to stiffen but not to completely set, then cut into circles with a cookie cutter. Reserve the chocolate scraps.

4 Finely chop the hazelnuts and almonds; set aside. Cut two parchment paper strips and place in a 1¾–2¼ l (1–2 qt) mold to make the dessert easier to unmold. Cut the cake in half horizontally; cut each layer in pieces to fit the bottom and sides of the mold. Line the mold with cake; then add 4–6 tbsp liqueur of your choice.

5 Melt the reserved chocolate scraps. Pour 600 ml (1 pt) cream into a bowl and whip. Mix in tiny chocolate drops, almonds, hazelnuts, vanilla, 2 tbsp powdered sugar and 2 tbsp liqueur. Mix well, then pour half into the mold and level off.

6 Add the melted chocolate to the other half, and pour this into the mold. Cover with a parchment paper circle. Chill for 4 hours or more.

7 Turn out the sponge onto a piece of parchment paper and remove the paper strips. Dust with the remaining powdered sugar. Sift powdered chocolate over the spaces and carefully remove the paper.

8 Put two spatulas underneath the cake and lift it onto a serving dish. Whip the remaining cream and pipe rosettes of cream around and on top of the cake. Decorate with chocolate powder and glacé cherries, if desired, and chill until ready to serve.

Venetian Fruit Cake

Serves 4

For the pastry

50 g (2 oz) fresh yeast
100 g (4 oz) sugar
300 ml (10 fl oz) lukewarm milk (35°C/95°F)
600 g (1 lb 6 oz) self-rising flour
100 g (4 oz) butter
3 egg yolks
grated zest of 1 lemon

For the filling

75 g (3 oz) hazelnuts, toasted, skins rubbed off
100 g (4 oz) chopped walnuts
65 g (2½ oz) golden raisins
120 ml (4 fl oz) rum
100 g (4 oz) butter
225 g (8 oz) superfine sugar
4 eggs, separated
250 ml (8 fl oz) whipping cream, whipped
grated zest of 1 lemon
pinch ground cinnamon
1 egg, beaten

1 For the pastry, crumble the yeast into a cup, add a pinch of salt, the sugar and lukewarm milk (reserving a few tbsp). Put the flour in a bowl, add the yeast mixture and half of the butter and mix well together.

2 Form the dough into a ball and put into a floured bowl. Cut a cross on the surface, cover the dough and leave to rise until doubled in size. Then add the egg yolks beaten with the reserved milk, the remaining butter cut into pieces and the grated lemon zest. Knead well, cover and leave to rise again. Then knock back, knead and leave to rise once more.

3 For the filling, chop the hazelnuts and mix with the walnuts. Soak the raisins in rum. Cream the butter with half of the sugar. Beat the egg yolks with the remaining sugar until frothy. Add to the butter–sugar mixture; fold in the whipped cream, lemon zest and cinnamon. Add the drained raisins and half of the chopped nuts.

4 Beat the egg whites until stiff and fold in. Roll out the dough on a floured board. Cut into three oblongs, the length of the baking sheet. Spread the filling onto these; sprinkle with the remaining nuts. Roll lengthways, brush with beaten egg and place on a greased baking sheet. Leave to rise for 15 minutes, then bake at 190°C/375°F/Gas Mark 5 for 1 hour.

Acknowledgements

The publishers would like to thank the following picture libraries for their kind permission to use their pictures:

Alamy: 5

Istock: 25, 48, 62, 75, 90, 109, 112, 144, 151

Shutterstock: 7, 9, 11, 15, 17, 18, 20, 21, 22, 29, 32, 33, 36, 39, 42, 44, 47, 49, 51, 53, 54, 55, 56, 57, 61, 66, 67, 68, 69, 70, 72, 74, 77, 78, 81, 82, 84, 85, 86, 88, 89, 91, 92, 93, 94, 96, 99, 100, 101, 102, 103, 104, 106, 110, 113, 114, 115, 116, 119, 120, 121, 122, 123, 127, 132, 134, 135, 136, 146, 148, 149, 162, 164, 165, 167, 168, 169, 170

Photocuisine: 63, 154, 158

Stockfood: front cover, 129, 137, 143, 148, 157

Every effort has been made to contact the copyright holders for images reproduced in this book. The Publisher would welcome any errors or omissions being brought to their attention and apologizes in advance for any unintentional omissions or errors. The Publisher will be pleased to insert the appropriate acknowledgement to any companies or individuals in any subsequent edition of the work.